William Caxton
A portrait in a background

EDMUND *Lunness* CHILDS

St. Martin's Press

New York

w

Library of Congress Catalog Card Number: 77-25770
First published in the United States of America in 1978

Library of Congress Cataloging in Publication Data

Childs, Edmund Lunness.
  William Caxton: a portrait in a background.

  Bibliography: p.
  Includes index.

  1. Caxton, William, 1422 (ca)-1491.

  2. Printers—England—Biography.

Z232.C38C5 1978   686.2′092′4   77-25770
ISBN 0-312-88068-5

For

BERNARD NELSON BESSUNGER

A devoted amateur of the graphic arts

"Go lytyl boke"

ACKNOWLEDGEMENTS

It would be impossible to name all the friends and colleagues who have assisted and encouraged me in writing this book, but I feel obliged to single out a few for special mention. Bernard Bessunger not only prompted me to start on it but thereafter prodded me constantly until I finished it. Stanley Greenwood and Clive Goodacre of Northwood Publications Ltd have made many suggestions in shaping the book, and I am grateful for the great help they have given since the day I first showed them a few tentative chapters. Frank Shore I must thank for doing much of the leg-work and library-haunting that was involved in researching the book, and also his daughter, Frances Smith, for her expert advice on medieval costume. James E. Johnson, a colleague at Her Majesty's Stationery Office, was most kind in loaning me his valuable first edition of Luckombe's *The Art and History of Printing* (1771) from which I have taken a quotation, and in reading the proofs with an experienced eye.

Acknowledgement is also due to the following for permission to reproduce certain of the illustrations in this book: the Public Record Office (plate I); the President and Fellows of Queens' College, Cambridge (plate II, portrait of Elizabeth Woodville); the Master and Fellows of Magdalene College, Cambridge (plate VI); Radio Times Hulton Picture Library (plates II, IV and V); Lambeth Palace Library (the illumination from MS 265 showing Earl Rivers presenting his *Dictes* to Edward IV, page 151); and St Bride Printing Library (the engraving on page 25 of an early printing-office in Haarlem). The illustrations of Caxton's typefaces are those used by William Blades in his *Biography and Typography of William Caxton* (1877), from which they are reproduced, as also are the examples of woodcuts and initial letters. What would I have done without dear William Blades?   E.L.C.

CONTENTS

ILLUSTRATIONS

PLATES
(between pages 80 and 81)

Foreword

The invention of printing gave new life to all branches of know-
ledge, and if we thoughtfully consider the wonderful effects which
have proceeded from it – effects far more important to mankind than
even the discovery of steam power, electric power, or any other
invention – we shall surely feel deeply interested in all that concerns
its introduction and spread in our own country.

So wrote William Blades in the preface to his monumental study of
England's first printer.[1] If Blades were alive today he would find
much greater marvels of technology than steam power and electric-
ity with which to compare printing – and still to printing's advantage. It was printing that gave man a new means of communicating
his ideas and of perpetuating them. Before the coming of printing
he could speak to bystanders or pen his thoughts in a manuscript.
Modern and more sophisticated media now enable him to reach a
much wider audience, but only in print can his ideas be transmitted
over the years, and the printed word remains the surest repository
of literature and learning. The Reformation thrust open the door to
the freedom of thought; the Renaissance extended the horizons of
knowledge; but without the art of printing, which grew up along
with them, these momentous movements could not have spread
and their effects would not have survived.

This country's debt to a printer has long been acknowledged. It is
five hundred years since William Caxton produced the first book
ever printed in the English language. His name is familiar to all of
us, but ironically, though it was he who provided the process

1. *The Biography and Typography of William Caxton*, 2nd ed. (Trübner, London:
1882).

13

whereby the story of his life could have been recorded, very little else is known of him. Beyond a few entries in musty archives, what we do know is what he tells us in some of his prologues and epilogues.

In the absence of facts, biographers of Caxton before Blades relied much on their fancy; some resorted almost to downright fiction. It is therefore to Blades that a new biographer will turn first when writing of Caxton. Any biographer, or historian in general, must necessarily rely largely on the researches of his predecessors and is after all little more than an editor. At the same time however he will weigh the worth of his sources with a critical hindsight. We know how Tudor apologists systematically blackened the character of Richard III and how Shakespeare was misled by Holinshed. If he goes back far enough and is so fortunate as to uncover what purports to be an eye-witness account of some distant event, this too he must scrutinise equally closely. It is notorious how eye-witnesses can colour their evidence with prejudice and some contemporary chroniclers of Caxton's times for all their propinquity are particularly unreliable. Warkworth's Chronicle of the first thirteen years of Edward IV's reign, which is pleasantly chatty and eminently readable, and the so-called Hearne's Fragment covering the years 1468 to 1482, are often at variance and both must be regarded with especial suspicion.[2] Even the autobiographical references in Caxton's own writings must sometimes be taken with a pinch of salt.

Certainly facts concerning Caxton's life are few and far between and there are gaps which we can hardly hope ever to fill in. But it cannot be supposed that on any subject the last word has already been spoken. The archives of the Mercers' Company and the registers of Westminster Abbey and of St Margaret's, Westminster, have been sifted thoroughly. Yet there remains the chance that among the mass of records and muniments that have come down to us we might still come across a gem like the Papal Indulgence discovered as late as February 1928 in the Public Record Office.

---

2. For the general reader an entertaining compendium of fifteenth-century chronicles, including Warkworth's Chronicle, Hearne's Fragment and other contemporary documents and letters, is provided by J. C. Giles, *The Chronicles of the White Rose of York* (London: 1843). A reprint (1974) is available from A. J. Sutton, 32A Rosebery Road, Dursley, Glos.

Such serendipity apart, Blades himself saw the need to update his original volumes. In his 1877 version[3] he was able to prove that Caxton was indeed married. His evidence was a document included in a collection of Exchequer Rolls which had been preserved in the Chapter House of Westminster Abbey and had just previously been handed over to the Public Record Office for collation and safe keeping. He also had access to a missing portion of the will of Robert Large, Caxton's master, which had been discovered in the Probate Registry of Somerset House. Regarding Large's will it is significant that although he mentions that the text he uses is translated from a book called "Rouse", he does not appear to have considered that the book might have been the work of John Rous, sometimes spelled Rouse, the garrulous fifteenth-century annalist who regarded nothing as unworthy of notice in his prolix recital of everyday occurrences throughout his long life. He was, incidentally, a close contemporary of Caxton and they died in the same year.

While acknowledging that Blades was an outstanding Caxton scholar and that his work provides the soundest foundation for any new study, it must be admitted that his grasp of the history of the fifteenth century, and of the intricacies of genealogy that arose from the feuding and intermarrying of the leading noble families, was somewhat uncertain and allows him to make curious errors occasionally. For instance[4] he plainly confuses Warwick the Kingmaker with the earl of Warwick to whom Caxton dedicated the first edition of his Chess book. By the time Caxton had translated this book and it had appeared in print (1475) the Kingmaker had been killed at the second battle of Barnet (1471), and both his earldom and most of his vast estates had devolved on Edward IV's younger brother, George duke of Clarence, who had married Warwick's daughter, Isabella. He makes a similar mistake in too easily identify-

---

3. Blades first published his work in two quarto volumes under the title *The Life and Typography of William Caxton* (London and Strassburg: Trübner, 1861–63). In 1877, to mark the Caxton quatercentennial celebrations, he issued a one-volume edition *The Biography and Typography of William Caxton*, of which a second edition appeared in 1882. A photo-litho reproduction of this was published in 1971 (London: Frederick Muller) with an introduction by James Moran, which summarises the points on which Blades has been superseded by more recent researchers. This is the edition referred to mainly in the present study, and is simply designated in any following notes as "Blades 1877".

4. Blades 1877, pp. 24, 28, 81.

ing Shakespeare's buffoonish creation, Falstaff, with the extremely literate and cultivated real-life Sir John Fastolf.[5]

This might seem mere carping. Blades was by training a master printer, not an academic, but from his early days his bent was towards the history of his craft and from the outset of his studies he appears to have been almost hypnotised by Caxton and his work. To make up for the lack of reliable earlier documentation, he concentrated perhaps too closely on searching for any oblique evidence he could find in any books printed by Caxton on which he could lay his hands. He examined some five hundred books known or reputed to have come from Caxton's press. The outcome was not so much a biography as a bibliography. It is in fact the bibliographical aspects of his work that are most valuable and though this was not his primary aim he was responsible for initiating much of what is now standard bibliographical practice.

Like many experts Blades was blinkered by his own specialism. It would be presumptuous for anyone to think he could displace Blades from his pinnacle in the field of Caxton studies. But it is reasonable and might be rewarding, even if we cannot directly add to his industrious researches, to subject his findings to a measure of re-appraisal.

If we employ what might be called a synoptic approach and observe Caxton against the colourful backcloth of his century, his shadowy outline might take on a firmer shape. A man is known by the company he keeps. Caxton was rich in friends and moved in influential circles. And beyond his immediate circle there were men who, even if he never met them, must have left their mark on his manner of life as also they have on the world at large. It was the century of Henry the Navigator, Columbus, Cabot and Bartholemew Diaz; Leonardo da Vinci and the Medici family; Erasmus and John Colet; and of Malory, Lydgate, Dunbar and Skelton – two of whom he put in print.

It was a bloody century too, torn constantly by wars, here in England by what have become known as the Wars of the Roses and on the Continent by the intermittant battles of the Hundred Years War. But it was more besides. Battles were not the apocalytic

---

5. Blades 1877, pp. 81, 189, 230.

struggles of modern times. They were fought by small armies of retainers and levies, and while kings and lords strove with each other for position and power, life for most people in England, though not unaffected by the flow of events around them, continued its course steadily. Peasants delved, craftsmen wrought, weavers made their cloth, and mercers and merchants like Caxton thrived.[6] From time to time poets raised their voices, scholars sought to illumine the minds of their fellows, and the Church, despite its widespread venality and involvement in matters of State, cared for their souls, as well as nurturing the New Learning. This was until reformers, most of them from among its own members, took over and challenged not only its religious authority but its leadership in the field of letters. It was above all the century in which a revolutionary means of communicating ideas was invented. Caxton was shrewd enough to recognise the importance of this novelty, at least for his immediate purposes, but cannot have realised how greatly it was to affect the lives of all men ever after.

In 1771 nearly a hundred years before Blades issued his two volumes an almost equally diligent work appeared. It was *The History and Art of Printing*, by P. Luckombe, an author too modest to spell out his forename. In a prefatory address "To the Public" he disarmingly says:

"The Editor of this Work prefumes to add, That he is not fo vain as to imagine he fhall be free from Inaccuracies, that his Opinion is always right, or his Abilities equal to the ufeful tafk he has undertaken: but hopes he fhall be treated with Candour. It is offending againft the Laws of Juftice and Charity, and even Decency and common Civility, to be pleafed with the difcovery of miftakes of Authors, when committed through inadvertency and multiplicity of concerns. It is the hardeft tafk in nature; nay, it is impoffible to pleafe all, however defirous and agreeable it might be, or let his intentions be ever fo praife-worthy."

6. G. M. Trevelyan, *English Social History* (Longman, London: 1944). Chapter III, "England in the Age of Caxton", is, as would be expected, a scholarly nut-shell account of the social and economic background of the period.

With due and similar modesty this present essay is offered. Its aim is the same as Luckombe's:

"We have endeavoured to make this book as useful as the limits that an Octavo Volume will permit of. Everything worthy of observation will be taken notice of, and a great number of curious and antique anecdotes relative to Printing introduced."

Westminster, 1975

INTRODUCTION

The Birth of Printing

Printing in the sense that most people think of it only became truly practicable, or even possible, when "movable type" was invented. Before then books and texts, though not a great number, had been printed from wood-blocks on which each line of letters making up a page had to be laboriously engraved in relief. This in its day was no doubt a notable advance as many more copies of a manuscript could be produced, and much more quickly, than had been possible by hand, but that was the limit of its usefulness. The earliest known book printed in this way is the *Diamond Sutra*, part of the Buddhist scriptures, which bears the statement "printed on 11 May 868 by Wang Chieh". Discovered in 1907 by Sir Aurel Stein in Tunhuang, Kansu, and now in the British Museum, it consists of six sheets of text each printed from separate blocks, and a wood-cut illustration, pasted together to make a roll sixteen feet long. The first real step forward in the mechanical reproduction of manuscripts was when the idea was conceived of casting letters of the alphabet as individual pieces of metal, which could be locked together, or "composed", to form the lines of printed sheets or the pages of a book and afterwards broken down or "distributed" for use in the same way again and again. Traditionally the credit for this is given to Johann Gensfleisch zum Gutenberg, a Mainz goldsmith, the date of whose birth has been put by some historians as early as 1394 and by others as late as 1406.

In point of fact the Chinese more than four hundred years before Gutenberg was born are known to have been printing with movable types of a kind, which they moulded in clay or carved on small blocks of hardwood. An obvious disadvantage facing the Chinese was that their language called for something like 30,000 separate and intricate ideographs to represent it in visual form, whereas

Quod cū audiſſet dauid:deſcendit in
preſidiū.Philiſtijm autem venientes
diffuſſi ſunt in valle raphaim.Et cō=
ſuluit dauid dūm dicens.Si aſcendā
ad philiſtijm·et ſi dabis eos ī manu
mea? Et dixit dūs ad dauid.Aſcende:
qa tradens dabo philiſtijm in manu
tua.Venit ergo dauid ad baalphara=
ſim:et percuſſit eos ibi et dixit.Diuiſit
dūs inimicos meos corā me:ſicut di=
uidunt aque.Propterea vocatū ē no
men loci illi9 baalpharaſim.Et reliq=
runt ibi ſculptilia ſua:q̄ tulit dauid et
viri ei9.Et addiderunt adhuc philiſti=
im ut aſcenderent:et diffuſſi ſūt ī valle
raphaim.Cōſuluit autē dauid dūm.
Si aſcendā cōtra philiſteos:ꝫ tradas
eos in manus meas?Qui rūdit.Nō
aſcendas cōtra eos ſed gira poſt tergū
corū:ꝫ venies ad eos ꜩaduūlo piroru.
Et cū audieris ſonitū clamoris gra=

Part of a column of Gutenberg's 42-line Bible (II Samuel 5: 17–24)
printed in Mainz, 1452–6.

European languages need an alphabet of only two dozen or so letters. Nonetheless, in the East the idea was pursued with a characteristic persistence. In 1390 the king of Korea ordered the establishment of a type foundry and by 1403 a set of as many as 100,000 characters had been cast in copper. These and a second fount of similar type produced in 1420 continued in use for the printing of books until 1544.

The claim that it was Gutenberg who developed the use of movable type in Europe has more than once been challenged and it is likely that he owed more than he admitted to the skill and ingenuity of his assistant Peter Schoffer. In any case it is well known that Gutenberg was only one among a number of innovators who at that time were seeking to create an "artificial script", as they called it. With this they hoped to improve on the slow and limited output of the monastic scribes and lay scriveners, whose pens had so far been the sole means of reproducing for the scholars and libraries of those days copies of original manuscripts and texts.

It was because Gutenberg and his immediate successors were so intent on inventing an "artificial script" that their typefaces so closely resembled the letter forms that had been developed over the centuries in the monasteries, and why they included so many of the ligatures, contractions and other "shorthand" tricks that the scribes had devised to save their time. The result was that the "incunabula" – the name given to books surviving from the period before 1500, when printing was in its "swaddling clothes" – looked much the same as the hand-written works of the professional copyists. This indeed was the aim of the first printers; they thought of their art as a way of supplementing the output of the scribes, not of supplanting them. There is the story, amusing but doubtless apocryphal, of how Johannes Fust, the hard-headed Mainz lawyer who saw the commerical possibilities of Gutenberg's venture and put money into it, was arrested in Paris when he tried to sell copies of the Gutenberg Bible as authentic manuscripts. It was not because the Parisians were outraged or regarded the copies as fakes, but because the Church authorities thought that he must surely be in league with the Devil to be able to produce so many books identical in every letter and point.

One of the contractions retained in the founts of type cut for the

Scheme of Caxton's type case as reconstructed by William Blades.

A	B	C	D	E	F	G	H	J	K	L	M	N	O	P	Q	R	S	T	V
ā	ꝧ	c̄	ꝺ	ē	fa	g	ħ	J	k	la	m	ŋ	ō	p	q	r	ſa	ta	v
ǣ	ba	ca	ꝫ	ee	fe	ꝗ	ha	i	j	le	m̄	r̄	x	ꝑ	q̄	ꝛ	ſo	te	ū
1	be	cc	da	ei	fi	ffl	he	ii	ÿ	ti	mi	n̄	or	p̄	ẞ	ꝛ	ſe	th	9
2	bo	ce	de	en	fl	ffo	ho	in	im	ll	lo	ni	°	ṗ	ꝗ	ra	ſh	ti	va
3	br	ci	do	eꞃ	fo	ffu	c	iŋ	im	tt	lu	nu	'	p̄	q́	re	ſi	to	ve
4		co	dr	er	fr	b	c	d	e	i	f	s		pa	un	ri	ſl	tr	vo
5		cr	W	æ	fu	m	n	y	o	a	h	ſ	:	pe	uꞃ	ro	ſo	tu	ſſ
6	Y	ct	w	eu	ff	u	r	t	l				/	po	uꞃ	rr	ſu	ſſi	ſſa
7	X	Z	wa	ex	ffa									pp	&	ru	ſſu	ſſo	ſſe
8	x	Z	we	eȝ	ffe								•	ẙ	ẙ	⊏			
9	o	3	wo	°	ffi									ẙ	ẙ	=			

En Quads and Spaces (central lower section); *Em Quads* (right lower section).

22

first English printers was y^e for *the*, which continued in use for centuries, and is still used affectedly to impart an archaic touch to a setting. Ligatures, or letters cast together on one body or shank of metal, like ff, fi, fl, ffi, ffl and a few others, deservedly survive – not only because these letters occur so frequently together, but because they make finer letterspacing possible. The earliest type designs were close imitations of the "gothic" letter forms penned by the scribes, along with all their ligatures and other calligraphic devices, which were adopted almost in their entirety – though much transformed – when "roman" and "italic" types came into being, not long after Gutenberg brought his experiments to a workable stage. The first roman types were cut in Strassburg in 1467, a year before Gutenberg died and were perfected in Venice by Nicholas Jenson, a Frenchman, in 1470. Italic type, supposedly based on the cursive handwriting of Petrarch, the sonneteer of a century before, was first used by Aldus Manutius the Venetian printer in 1501 for his edition of Virgil's *Aeneid*.

It was in italic founts that ligatures were most prolific, because owing to the slope of the letters many of them could not be set close enough together if they were cast separately. Some founts, both in italic and roman, were so faithful to their manuscript originals that they contained as many as fifty joined letters of this sort. This predilection for ligatures died hard and some old style founts revived in the late nineteenth century brought back the ligatures ct and st in which the letters are connected by a totally unnecessary curved stroke – intended again, no doubt, to provide an antique look.

The abbreviation most familiar to all of us is the ampersand (&) which has been traced back to the Rome of the first century BC and which today, two thousand years later, is still accepted as a sign for the word *and* in languages that employ the Roman alphabet. It was formed by combining the two letters of the Latin word *et* into one symbol, though in later versions of it even the most discerning eye will find it difficult to distinguish the *e* and the *t*. Some typefounders, including modern ones, have given the ampersand a florid, pretentious appearance that quite belies its original stenographic purpose and though it has persisted to this day typographical designers make sparing use of it, and very rarely, in text matter.

In Gutenberg's day and for a long time afterwards, the "case" or box-like receptacle from which printers pick up pieces of type for composing a job had compartments for over two hundred different letters, ligatures and abbreviations. Over the years most of the ligatures and abbreviations have been discarded in the cause of simplicity and rationalisation, and today the compositor makes do with far fewer "sorts" or characters. Originally the compositor's case consisted of a single frame holding all the sorts making up a set of type and was tilted at an angle to give easier access to the upper compartments which held the capital letters.

Later it was realised that to use two smaller cases, one above the other, assisted the compositor even more in reaching for the various pieces, and a further improvement came when letters that occur most often in combination with others were placed in adjacent compartments. As capital letters are required less frequently than small letters they are still kept in the upper case, while small letters are in the lower and nearer case. Printers nowadays, perhaps to mystify the layman, refer to the letters themselves as "upper case" and "lower case".

What especially aided Gutenberg in his experiments and enabled him to outdo his contemporaries was that he was particularly skilled in the art of engraving and the science of metallurgy, both of which were necessary adjuncts of his trade as a goldsmith. Since ancient times goldsmiths and other metal workers had been entrusted with the engraving of dies for the striking of medals and coins, but for this purpose it was normally necessary to make only one die. To cut the alphabet one by one in the thousands that are required for the composing of a book was obviously an impossible undertaking. A way of mass-producing type was needed, and it was in devising a method of doing this that Gutenberg showed his true inventiveness. He realised that if he first made a series of steel punches, one for each letter of the alphabet, these if hardened, could be used for striking in a softer metal such as brass, a reverse matrix or "female" die, from which any number of identical pieces of type could be cast.

Apart from the probability that he was given valuable technical assistance by Peter Shoffer in developing movable type, at one time a serious contender for Gutenberg's title was Laurensz Jansz Coster

An early printing-office in Haarlem, home of Laurensz Jansz Coster, once thought to be the inventor of movable types. In the background a compositor is setting type from the inclined cases. This is thought to be the first accurate representation of a printing-office and is from a Dutch book published in 1628, the title of which can be translated as *Description and Praise of the Town of Haarlem*.

An early printing press, from a German *Book of Trades* (1568). One printer is
removing a printed sheet and the second is inking the type forme with "ink-balls"
ready for the next impression. In the background compositors are setting type.

of Haarlem (1405–84). In 1771 Luckombe[1] recorded that some inhabitants of Haarlem still asserted that their city, not Mainz, was the birthplace of Western printing. Movable type they said was the brain-child not of Gutenberg, but of Coster, who after first printing with wood-blocks hit upon the notion in the year 1430 of cutting single letters in steel and then striking them into copper to form a matrix. Gutenberg was said to have been Coster's assistant and was alleged to have stolen Coster's tools while his master was in church and to have made off with them to Mainz. The "Coster legend", which in any case was not put about until 1568, has long since been discredited by Dutch scholars, but as Steinberg[2] reflects, "the monuments erected in Coster's honour by his townsmen will no doubt keep the myth alive among such people as will believe that Bacon wrote Shakespeare". Almost a century later in 1664 the story was resurrected in England, when an attempt was made by the forger, Richard Atkyns, to deprive Caxton of his crown as England's first printer.[3]

An undisputed instance of Gutenberg's genius was his design for a mould that could be adjusted to hold matrices of varying widths, narrow letters like *i* or broader letters like *m*, thereby avoiding the gap-toothed effect that would occur in a word if all type were cast to the same width. Moulds similar to Gutenberg's, though of a later date, in the possession of the University Press at Oxford, are still in working order. They are made in two parts, which after the selected matrix has been fitted between them, can be clamped firmly together leaving open an orifice about an inch deep into which molten metal can be poured to form a shank or "body", with the letter that has been punched in the matrix standing out in relief on the lower end of it.

Nor does our indebtedness to Gutenberg end there. His expert knowledge of metallurgy enabled him to develop a special alloy for casting his type – a mixture of lead, tin and antimony – which would fuse easily and flow readily into the mould yet would be

---

1. P. Luckombe, *The History and Art of Printing* (London: 1771).
2. S. H. Steinberg, *Five Hundred Years of Printing* (Pelican Books, London: 1955).
3. *The Original and Growth of Printing, collected out of History and the Records of this kingdom: wherein is also demonstrated, that Printing appertaineth to the Prerogative Royal, and is a Flower of the Crown of England.* By Richard Atkyns, Esq; London, 1664.

tough and hard-wearing when it set. These three ingredients are used to this day in making type metal.

Gutenberg's inventiveness did not however extend to the designing of a press to be used especially for printing. As James Moran has pointed out,[4] all that the early printers did was to adapt the already existing and well-known domestic screw press, and though Gutenberg may have introduced some innovations to make this more suitable for his purpose, these cannot have been considerable. The mechanics of the printing press did not change greatly in the course of almost four hundred years.

Gutenberg's ideas took but a few years to irradiate from his native Mainz, and presses were soon set up in most of the important cities of Europe – at Cologne in 1464, Rome in 1467, Venice in 1469, Paris in 1470, Milan and Florence in 1471, Budapest in 1473, and even distant Cracow in 1474 – to name only some. It was in Cologne, where he lived between 1470 and 1472, that William Caxton, whose life-span overlapped that of Gutenberg by some forty-five years, received his first lessons in the art of printing and became "the father of English printing".

---

4. J. Moran, *Printing Presses: History and Development from the Fifteenth Century to Modern Times* (Faber and Faber, London: 1973).

CHAPTER 1

Family Background

In his prologue to *The Recuyell of the Historyes of Troye*, the first book that Caxton translated and the first book ever printed in the English language, he tells us: "I was born and lerned myn englissh in Kente in the Weeld, where I doubte not is spoken as brode and rude englissh as in ony part of englond." Though we have been advised against taking too literally anything that Caxton says of himself it would seem reasonable at least to accept his word that he was born in Kent and to conclude that if he learned his English there he spent some of his childhood years there also. When he refers to the "brode and rude englissh" of the Weald, and in the same prologue to his "sympleness and unperfightness" in French ("for in France was I never"), though he may be observing the literary convention which required early authors to deprecate their personal accomplishments – the "humility formula", as it has been called – he also presents us with as definite a starting point as we can hope for in our enquiries into his life.

A more exact location for his birthplace has never been satisfactorily established. Various places in Kent have been nominated, but the arguments in support of any of them are far from convincing. One of the most favoured is the village of Hadlow, four miles north-east of Tonbridge. Its champions, Blades among them, contend that Caxton came of a family who were once lords of the manor of Caustons, which was part of the parish of Hadlow. For this the evidence adds up to little more than that the name Caustons is a variant of Caxton – which indeed it is. It is but one of a dozen or more spellings of the name that are to be found in numerous documents and records dating from the fifteenth century and earlier. Other common examples are Cawston, Cauxton, Cacston, Caxston and Caxtone. As spelling in those days, and much later, had no firm rules, this is not surprising and the name appears in one form or another not only in Kent, but even more often in London and also as far north as Norwich and Nottingham. Sometimes two different spellings are used in the same document, as in the records of the Mercers' Company, where one of the liverymen appointed to welcome Edward IV on his entry into London to claim the throne in 1461 is referred to first as Thomas Cacston and a few lines further on as Thomas Cawston.[1]

In all examples of his work that carry his imprint Caxton himself uses the now accepted spelling. This might be said to undermine the theory that he was one of the Hadlow Caustons. For instance, in *The Dictes and Sayings of the Philosophers*, the first full scale book to come from his press after he returned to England, he says: "Enprynted by me William Caxton at Westmestre the yere of our lord Mcccclxxvii". He occasionally uses *y* instead of *i* in his forename, but his surname always appears as Caxton. On the other hand Wynken de Worde, his foreman and successor, in works published after Caxton's death, though he refers to his master only eight times, uses four different versions – Caxton, Caxston, Caston and Caxon – the last two being yet further mutations to vex us. If so many variations were in common use Caxton's consistency in the spelling of his name is perhaps not so conclusive after all. Whatever his own preference might have been the first authenticated mention of him anywhere (the entry in the Mercers' records of his being apprenticed in 1438[2]) calls him Caxston, though in all subsequent entries he becomes Caxton. Later when he had settled at Westminster the same two variants are used in the registers of St Margaret's, where he was an honoured parishioner.

Today the village of Hadlow retains nothing, apart from the parish church, of the medieval features it would have had in Caxton's time. The first church was built probably of wood in 975 and

---

1. Blades 1877 p. 3. In an appendix (pp. 143–64) Blades reprints all the relevant entries in the Wardens' Accounts of the Mercers' Company that concern Caxton and some of his contemporaries and possible antecedents. Written in the varying hands of successive clerks on parchment, the entries are dated by the regnal year of the king of the time; the volume Blades gives extracts from covers the years 1344–1464. These and other archives of the Company are preserved at Mercers' Hall, Ironmonger Lane, London EC2, having survived the destruction of earlier halls in the Great Fire of London, 1666, and in the bombing of London in World War II.

2. Blades 1877 p. 146.

fragments of the present fabric date from 1018, when Queen Eddeva, wife of Edward the Confessor, is thought to have rebuilt the church in stone. The parish registers are complete from 1558 and in good condition, but naturally are of no help in tracing Caxton's antecedents. The list of vicars of Hadlow is also intact, except for 1422, the more generally accepted year of Caxton's birth, when by ironic coincidence a new incumbent is shown simply as "William S- - - -". In the immediate vicinity of the church are some pleasant timbered Elizabethan houses, but otherwise the only objects worthy of architectural notice are a derelict Victorian brewery built to process the local hops, and an octagonal Gothic folly which rears its pinnacles to a height of 170 feet and is visible from miles around. It was erected in 1840 by an eccentric squire, William Barton May, who inherited land, married money and assumed heraldic arms to which he had no right. The story goes that he built it to see over the trees to neighbouring Fishall where his estranged wife lived. For the most part the present inhabitants of Hadlow appear to regard the possibility that their village was the birthplace of Caxton with a buccolic indifference and in a brochure published to mark the millennium of the parish church in 1975 the honour is as nearly as can be abrogated in favour of nearby Tenterden.

Tenterden's claim to be the birthplace of Caxton is hardly more substantial than that of Hadlow. This did not prevent the editors of the Dictionary of National Biography, when they published a volume of errata which they gave away to subscribers to this enormous "parts publication", from adding the purely gratuitous note that he was born "at Tenterden". There was certainly a Thomas Caxton who was a lawyer and a man of means living at Tenterden in 1439. But the supposition that he was the brother of Caxton the printer, which has been put forward, is quite groundless.[3] A telling point against it is that in 1416–17 this Thomas was already well established and paid a tax of ten shillings (a large sum in those days) on property he had. If he were the printer's brother he must have

---

3. W. J. B. Crotch, *The Prologues and Epilogues of William Caxton* (London: Oxford University Press, 1928, for the Early English Text Society). In the invaluable "Biographical Introduction" to this volume, which occupies about one-half its pages, Crotch examines (pp. xxxii–xxxvi) Thomas Caxton's possible connection with William Caxton as some length. Like Blades, Crotch is an indispensable work of reference for Caxton students, and hereafter in this book is cited simply as "Crotch 1928".

been the elder by many years. He would in fact have been old enough to be the printer's father. But again there is no evidence of any sort to support this supposition either.

Any attempt to link William Caxton with Tenterden is as dubious as it is for any other place and nobody should be misled by the fact that there is a public-house called the William Caxton there. Until about 1940 it was the Black Horse. But the Tenterden tradition dies hard. In 1951 as part of the Festival of Britain observances this small township in the Weald exhibited what were described as "The Caxton Charters", implying that Caxton was indeed one of its sons. These charters, seventeen of them, which were found in 1922 at Shillinglee Park, the home of Lord Winterton, and are now in the British Museum, largely concern a family who lived in Little Wratting in Suffolk – a far cry from Tenterden. The charters show that a Philip Caxton, who acquired the lordship of the manor of Little Wratting about the year 1420, had two sons – Philip, born in 1412, and William, born about 1415. As the birth of William Caxton the printer has been set by some writers as early as 1415, it has been suggested that he and the second son of Philip Caxton of Little Wratting were the same person. By itself this stretches coincidence rather far. But in the third charter a deed of sale by the younger Philip Caxton is recorded as having been sealed by two London merchants, Thomas Cateworthe and Robert Large. Robert Large we shall meet in the next chapter as the mercer to whom Caxton the printer is known to have been apprenticed in 1438. This certainly must be coincidence, because if Caxton the printer was the son of the elder Philip Caxton and was born in 1415, in 1438 he would have been twenty-three, years too old to be just entering on his apprenticeship.

In the twelfth charter another coincidence confuses the issue yet further. A grant of land is recorded as having been made to Benedict Burgh, an East Anglian priest who later became a canon at Westminster and whose translation of Cato was one of the earlier productions of Caxton's press. At the time he made his translation Burgh was vicar of Malden, in Essex, and it was to Essex, according to Blades,[4] that some of the Caustons had moved from Hadlow in Kent, and had named their new home Hadlow Hall. If this is so

---

4. Blades 1877 p. 3.

Timbered Elizabethan houses in Church Street, Hadlow, with the medieval parish
church and Squire May's gothic folly in the background.

B

(and Blades cites the will of Johannes Cawston of Hadlow Hall, Essex, dated 1490, to support it, with little regard for the gap of years), it could be that Burgh was acquainted with both the Caxtons of Little Wratting, as his name in the charters indicates, and with the Cawstons of Hadlow Hall, Essex. The two families could, moreover, have been related. But to proceed from this to identify William Caxton of Westminster with William Caxton of Little Wratting is pure speculation.[5] The most we can deduce from the Caxton Charters is that it was perhaps not by mere chance that Benedict Burgh came to know Caxton at Westminster and prevailed on him to publish his *Cato*. And even this is tenable only if we accept with Blades that the Essex Cawstons were in some way connected with the Caxtons of Kent and in particular with the Caxtons of Hadlow rather than of Tenterden.

As we have observed, though we may accept Caxton's word that he was born in Kent, when he says "in the Weald" he may have been subscribing to the "humility formula" in order to excuse to his well-born patrons and readers his "brode and rude englissh". In the same way John Lyly, the Elizabethan whose mannered prose was certainly not "brode and rude" and gave us the word euphuism, admits that he too was "borne in the wylde of Kent". This is surely an atrocious and deliberate pun rather than another example of the vagaries of English spelling, and indicates that the Weald was then regarded as an uncultivated and uncivilised area. So much so it has been argued, that Caxton's family, who must have been of some standing for him to become a member of the most influential livery company in London, would hardly have lived in the Weald itself, at a small village such as Hadlow, or even at Tenterden, but more likely would have been residents of the county capital, Canterbury.

Like other places, Canterbury had its share of Caxtons. They included a William Caxton, a mercer who is recorded as being a freeman of that city in 1431 and therefore qualifies in terms of time as yet another candidate for the future printer's father. About the

---

5. A detailed discussion of the charters and abstracts from them will be found in N. F. Blake, *Willaim Caxton and Suffolk* (Proceedings of the Suffolk Institute of Archaeology, xxix, 2, 1962, pp. 139–53), and *William Caxton and Suffolk: A Supplement* (ibid., xxx, 1, 1964, pp. 112–15).

same period Robert Caxton, also a mercer, left considerable property in the parish of St Alphege, Canterbury. That is almost the extent of the Canterbury connexion, though it can be added that William Pratt, the prosperous London mercer who later was a patron of Caxton's press, and whom Caxton in the prologue to *The Book of Good Manners* describes as "a singular friend", was also a native of Canterbury.

The truth is that Caxtons were almost as numerous as Smiths are today; families of that ilk abounded everywhere and the majority of them were mercers. Among the 101 liverymen who are listed in the Mercers' records as having paid their annual dues in 1348 (22 Edw. 3), seven of them are named de Causton. Originally the name would appear to have been a placename, as the *de* which often precedes it indicates. In Domesday Book, Caxton in Cambridgeshire is referred to as Caustons. On the basis of this, while we may concede that a family of Caustons could have held the manor of a similar name near Hadlow in Kent, there is nothing to support the Blades hypothesis that they were ancestors of Caxton the printer.

In London Caxtons and Caustons were particularly prolific, long before Edward III invited Flemish weavers to settle in Kent and build up the wool trade for him. In 1303 Aubin de Causton, a haberdasher, was on a committee set up to enquire into the manufacture of caps using materials and methods forbidden by law – an early example of government intervention in industry. Four years later William de Causton was one of the City dignitories who signed a letter to the Bishop of Chester. In 1311 William de Caxtone had a house in the parish of St Mary Abchurch. The clan must for the most part have been a respected lot, for in 1327 John de Causton, an alderman, sat on a board of arbitrators appointed to settle a trade dispute. But there were some who were not so high in the social scale. John de Caxton and Thomas de Caxton were mere tradesmen, butchers in fact, and in 1331 the latter had his meat confiscated because his stall in the Poultry obstructed the street. In 1364 the family name was further besmirched when Alice de Causton, wife of a vintner, was sentenced to the "thewe" for thickening the bottom of a quart pot with pitch and giving short measure.

The forename William would appear to have been a popular one among the Caxtons. So no definite relationship should be assumed between the William de Causton, of the parish of St Vedast, who became an alderman in 1334 and was presumably by then a man of mature years, and the mercer of that name who was among the seven de Caustons who are mentioned above as having paid their livery fees in 1348. There are however, good circumstantial grounds for supposing that the latter was the same person as a William de Causton who was a wealthy mercer and died in 1354 – and for supposing that he represents the "missing link" in the descent of William Caxton, England's first printer, who was himself a mercer at the start of his business life.

Some eighty years ago at Westminster Abbey a large collection of documents were discovered concerning this William de Causton and extensive properties he owned, mainly in Edmonton, Enfield and Tottenham. How the documents came to be in the Abbey was a mystery, but Dr Edward J. L. Scott, who found them and was later Keeper of the Muniments at Westminster, made the perfectly plausible suggestion that they had been passed down through generations of one family and eventually came into the hands of William Caxton the printer, who for the last fifteen years of his life had close associations with the Abbey. Supporting Scott's suggestion is the fact that a Richard Caxton, who it is thought was probably related to the printer, became a monk at Westminster in 1473 and later from 1501 to 1503 was Treasurer of the Abbey.[6] If the monk and the printer were in fact related it is possible that in 1491, when William Caxton died without a male heir, the documents were put in the keeping of Dom Richard Caxton and when in turn he also died, in 1504, they were put away among the Abbey muniments simply because nobody came forward to claim them.

Two of the documents are of a later date than 1354 and belong to the reign of Richard II. In them we find the names of Henry and Nicholas de Causton, who are among the seven who along with William de Causton paid their livery fees in 1348. There also occurs the name of a John de Causton. From their context in the documents these three were all evidently contemporaries of the William of the earlier documents and in view of this the identification of the William de Causton of the Mercers' archives with the William de Causton of the Abbey muniments is as good as confirmed. But the

---

6. E. H. Pearce, *The Monks of Westminster* (Cambridge: 1916), p. 165.

two later documents principally concern a William Causton – without the *de* – who from internal evidence would appear to have been a son of the mercer who died in 1354. Pursuing his theory as to how these Caxton family papers ended up in the Abbey, Scott concluded that the two later documents had been added to the collection by the printer himself. He further ventured to identify this William Causton with a William Causton who was apprenticed to Thomas Gedeney, mercer, in 1401,[7] and him in turn with a William Causton who according to the Hustings Rolls of the City of London died before 1406.[8]

In this he was plainly in error as the two documents specifically belong to the reign of Richard II, who was murdered in 1399. And when he goes on to suggest that William de Causton who died in 1354 was the grandfather of Caxton the printer he appears to miss out a generation. If the Causton of the two later documents was the son of William de Causton who died in 1354, that would make him the father of the printer. But this he could not have been if he died in 1406. In any case the apprentice of 1401 could not have been the man who died in 1406; as an apprentice he could not have voted in elections, and would not have been in the Hustings Rolls.

Chronologically it is more likely that if the original William de Causton who died in 1354 was an ancestor of William Caxton he was his great-grandfather, while the William Causton who died in 1406 was his grandfather, and William Causton who was apprenticed in 1401 was his father. From this the possibility arises that the third of these Williams, the one apprenticed in 1401, was the William Caxton whose burial in 1478 is recorded in the churchwardens' accounts of St Margaret's, Westminster, and who has been assumed by earlier biographers (such as Dibdin,[9] but not Blades) to have been the father of Caxton the printer.

As recently as 1957 Lawrence E. Tanner, then Keeper of the Muniments at Westminster Abbey, said categorically: "It is also

---

7. Blades 1877 p. 145. Crotch 1928, p. xxxii, gives this entry as 1341 – presumably a printer's error.

8. Guildhall Record Office: Roll 134.

9. T. F. Dibdin, *Typographical Antiquities* (London: 1810).

not without significance that Caxton's father was living in Westminster when his son set up his printing-press . . .".[10] For that
matter the printer too was buried in St Margaret's, and though that
may be a coincidence the community of Westminster cannot have
been so great that it included many families all with the name of
Caxton. However, from various City records it seems that a youth
could not be indentured before he was fourteen years old. The
William Causton apprenticed in 1401 must therefore have been
born in 1387 or earlier. If he served a term of seven, or even ten,
years he could have issued from his apprenticeship by 1411 at the
latest and allowing a number of years for him to establish himself
he could have been married and a parent by 1422 – the date roughly
when the printer was born. The only snag is that if he and the man
who died in 1478 were the same person, and Caxton's father, he
would have been an ancient of about ninety, a remarkable age for
those times when longevity was unusual.

Although, as we have remarked, William was common as a
forename among the Caxtons, there is of course no reason to suppose that the printer's father was so named. But we can take it for
granted that he was a mercer and that his son followed in his
footsteps. So could he have been the Stevyn Causton who was a
paid-up liveryman of the Mercers' Company in 1424 (2 Hen. 6)?[11]
If so he was a close contemporary of Robert Large, who in 1428 (6
Hen. 6) became one of the four Wardens of the Company ("gar-
deins de la mistere del mercerie") and a few years later was to
become Caxton's master. We have no other record of Stevyn Causton, but that he knew Large intimately as a fellow mercer is a
reasonable conjecture.

He fulfils the essential requirements as Caxton's putative father
far better than most of those so far discussed, inasmuch as he was of
the right age and in a position to place his son in service with
Robert Large – the one substantiated piece of information that we
have concerning the young Caxton. The fact that he is named
Causton in the Mercers' records and Large's apprentice is named
Caxston presents no obstacle to this thesis, for though the printer

---

10. L. E. Tanner, *William Caxton's Houses at Westminster,* (a paper read before the
Bibliographical Society on 21 February 1956, and published in The Library, 5th
series, xii, 3 September 1957, pp. 153–66).
11. Wardens' Accounts, Mercers' Hall; Blades 1877 p. 145.

himself invariably used the form Caxton, archivists, parish clerks and other officials were not bound by any set rules in their spelling.

One question that remains unresolved if Caxton's father was a London mercer is how Caxton came to be born in Kent, as we have accepted. On reflection a possible answer is this. In those days the practice was for prominent citizens to apprentice their sons to one another and to restrict entry to the "mystery" of their particular livery companies in much the same way as some modern trade unions limit their membership. Caxton's father must himself therefore have been a man of some substance for his son to be accepted into the houschold of Robert Large, one of the leading City magnates, who was later to become mayor – an honour which required its holders, then as today, to dig deep into their own pockets during their tenure of office. It follows that besides having business connexions in London and possibly a "town residence" there, he could have owned land in Kent, whether at Hadlow, Tenterden, Canterbury or anywhere else, and that his son could not only have been born in Kent, but could also have spent some of his childhood there and learned the English which he felt obliged to belittle in his prologue to the *Recuyell*.

This is the proposition with which we started. To summarise, we can agree that Caxton was born in Kent, though not necessarily in the Weald. We can accept that his father, besides having a home in Kent, must have been a well-placed mercer in London. But who he was we cannot say with any confidence. The one original, if modest, contribution we have made, that there are possible grounds for believing him to have been Stevyn Causton has at least the virtue of novelty and is no more outrageous than other suggestions that have been put forward.

CHAPTER 2

The Mercer's Apprentice

Caxton first appears on the historical scene with an entry in the Wardens' Accounts of the Mercers' Company for the year 16 Hen. 6 (1438), which reads:

Item	John Large		les appñtices	
Item	Will'm Caxston	}	de Robert Large	iiijs

On the basis of this elaborate attempts have been made to calculate the year of Caxton's birth. Before Blades this had been generally assumed to be around 1412, because in about 1473 in the epilogue to Book III of the *Recuyell*, he wrote that age was creeping on him daily. This however should not be taken literally. It was probably an extension of the "humility formula" and he was excusing himself for committing his translation to print, as his eyes "were dimmed with overmuch looking on white paper", for which reason he had "practised and learnt, at great charge and expense, to ordain this said book in print, after the manner and form as we there see it, and not written with pen and ink as other books be". From this confession of his failing sight it was argued that he must have been at least sixty.

Blades considered that 1412 was far too early to be the year Caxton was born.[1] His reasoning is rather involved. He maintained that apprentices could not "issue" before they had reached the age of twenty-four and that the customary term of service was from seven to fourteen years, the most usual being ten years if we take the Mercers' records as a guide. He then proceeds, with no apparent justification: "if we calculate his servitude to have lasted but seven years, Caxton could not have been more than seventeen years of age when apprenticed, and would therefore have been born not later than the year 1421". Walter Besant, a better antiquary than historian, is much more direct on the subject. "He (Caxton) was

---

1. Blades 1877 p. 5.

born, I am sure, in the year 1424. It seems very clear that the usual age of apprenticeship was fourteen; and Caxton was certainly apprenticed in the year 1438, and since the year of admission to the City freedom was twenty-four, ten years were passed in servitude . . ."[2]

N. F. Blake challenges Blades' assertion (and by implication Besant's) that twenty-four was the age at which apprentices gained their freedom.[3] Blades had based his contention on an Act of Common Council passed in 1693, which required the City Chamberlain to ascertain that every candidate for admission to the freedom of the City had "reached the full age of twenty-four". Professor Blake points out that though an earlier Act of Common Council passed in the 1550s imposes a similar requirement, its implication is that an apprentice should be *not less* than twenty-four when he issued. In commenting that he has found no similar decree for the fifteenth century he is perhaps being too severe on Blades. That some such rule existed in the time of Caxton is to be seen from Robert Large's will, in which he stipulates that the bequests he makes to his sons are to be held in trust until they each "shall arrive at the age of twenty-four years", and as Blades says: "The phrase 'quousque ad etatem suam xxiiij annorum pervenerit', so commonly found in old wills, refers to this custom."[4]

When he questions whether Caxton was in fact apprenticed in 1438, as has always been pre-supposed from the entry in the Mercers' records, Professor Blake is perhaps again being too exacting. "The Account Book is," he writes, "as its name implies, a record of payments to and by the company; it is not a record of when apprentices were enrolled or issued. A master was supposed to pay the fee as soon as his apprentice was enrolled, but payment was not made promptly. Large was no exception." From a comparison of the dates of entry into and issue from apprenticeship that are given in the Mercers' books, this may well be a valid inference. "Consequently," he adds, "although Caxton had started his apprenticeship by 1438, it is not necessary to assume that he became an apprentice in that year." But the assumption that in every case the payment of fees was delayed seriously, or specifically in Caxton's case, would be equally dubious. Either Professor Blake is indulging in a little playful sophistry, or has for once fallen into the error that he rightly

---

2. Walter Besant, *Westminster* (Chatto and Windus, London: 1895) p. 171.

3. N. F. Blake, *Caxton and his World* (Andre Deutsch, London: 1969) pp. 22–24.

4. Blades 1877 pp. 5 and 151.

warns others against, namely of reading too much into too little evidence. While we cannot be sure that Caxton became an apprentice actually in the year 1438, neither can we be sure that he did not. What we can be certain of is that he became an apprentice *not later* than 1438, as that was the year in which Robert Large paid the required enrolment fee of two shillings each in respect of Caxton and of his own son, John Large. Admittedly there is the possibility that this payment was post-dated and that Caxton had already entered on his apprenticeship at some unspecified time earlier. But for all practical purposes we can take it that Caxton became an apprentice either in 1438 or maybe a year or two before. And that gives us an acceptable datum in attempting to decide what was the most likely year of his birth.

To do this we need to arrive first at an idea of what age Caxton would be when he entered Robert Large's service. That he was fourteen, as Besant boldly declares, has a fairly sound basis; a number of entries in the Plea and Memoranda Rolls of the City covering this period indicate clearly that it was not legal to bind as an apprentice a boy under fourteen.[5] If Caxton was only just fourteen when he was apprenticed in 1438, he would have been born, as Besant decided, in 1424. If he was apprenticed a year or two earlier, the date of his birth would be 1423 or 1422. If, as Blades argues (though from premises that are not well founded), he could not have been more than seventeen when apprenticed, he would have been born in 1421. However, bearing in mind Professor Blake's reservations regarding the year 1438, it might be necessary to put the year of his birth back still further| – but surely not to 1412. Professor Blake cautiously leaves it that Caxton "was born between 1415 and 1424".[6] An objection to either 1412 or 1415 as the year of Caxton's birth is that in 1438, or even a few years earlier, he would have been into his twenties – and much too old to be just starting his apprenticeship.

Summing up, if we follow Besant and accept that Caxton was apprenticed in 1438 at the earliest legal age of fourteen, he would have been born in 1424 – and that gives us the latest possible year for his birth. On the other hand, if we accept with Blades that Caxton was seventeen in 1438, he could indeed have been born in 1421. In point of fact it must be observed that Blades's exact words

---

5. Arthur H. Thomas, *Calendar of Plea and Memoranda Rolls 1413–1437* (University Press, Cambridge: 1943) and Philip E. Jones, *Calendar of Plea and Memoranda Rolls 1437–1457* (University Press, Cambridge: 1954).
6. op. cit. p. 25.

are that Caxton could not have been *more* than seventeen when apprenticed. If this distinction is taken in conjunction with the stipulation that legally he could not have entered service before he was fourteen, it follows that although the record in the Mercers' Account Book might have been post-dated, it could not have been so by more than three years. In other words he could have been fourteen – and 1421 still holds good as the earliest possible year of his birth. In spite of our pedantic obfuscations it looks as if Blades has been vindicated, and as if after all we must agree with him "that we cannot be far wrong if we assume 1422 –3 as the date of his (Caxton's) birth."

At whatever age William Caxton came to London to be apprentice-bound, the new circumstances and environment in which the young country lad found himself must have been strange and fascinating. The City merchants of that time were organised in exclusive fraternities. The Mercers' Company, of which Caxton's master, Robert Large, had long been one of the chief officers and of which Caxton himself was to become an honoured member in due course, was the oldest, most powerful and most prosperous of these ancient trade guilds. The manufacture and sale of cloth had from the reign of Edward III, a century before, been the principal industry of England and the basis of an extensive export trade.

The Mercers, who are still the premier livery company of the City of London, grew from a guild of vendors of silks and velvets, though later they extended their dealings to almost any kind of textiles and were not above dealing in other commodities if there was a profit to be made. They are first mentioned as a guild in 1172 and received their charter in 1394. From this same guild the Company of Merchant Adventurers was formed in 1296 and until the beginning of the sixteenth century the transactions of both were recorded in the same books. The Adventurers were mainly concerned with the development of the English cloth trade with Europe in the fourteenth century and their principal foreign staple, or depot, was established in 1344 in Bruges. Years later in 1463, William Caxton would be appointed Governor of this important body in all its dealings in the Low Countries and spend many years there.

Among early mercers can be mentioned Gilbert à Becket, father of St Thomas à Becket, who was martyred in Canterbury Cathedral in 1170. Another was Dick Whittington, "thrice mayor of London", who died about the year that Caxton was born.

Though best known as a hero of pantomime, in which he is depicted as a poor boy who made good, Whittington was the son of a Gloucestershire knight. With a small ship called appropriately the *Cat*, he plied his trade with the Continent, and advanced himself sufficiently to be able to make frequent loans to Henry IV and Henry V. His gifts to the City and to charity were munificent. In his will he left "good and rare books" to "the common library at Guildhall, for the profit of students there, and those discoursing to the common people".[7]

Less well known is Sir Henry Colet, twice mayor in Caxton's time and father of John Colet, who spent the greater part of the fortune his father left in endowing St Paul's School, which was originally in the City. Born about 1467, Colet could well have known Caxton, his father's fellow mercer, even if only slightly. Though he was only twenty-four when Caxton died, he had already won a reputation as a scholar and would certainly have been aware of Caxton's enterprise at Westminster and would have realised the effect that the art of printing would have on future educational methods. He was not able to use Caxton's press, but he was partly responsible for the issue in 1513 of William Lily's *Latin Grammar*, another edition of which was printed in 1527 by Caxton's successor, Wynkyn de Worde, one of the first publishers to recognise the lucrative market that the constant demand for schoolbooks was to represent. Something like two-thirds of de Worde's entire output was for the use of grammar-school boys. His foresight paid off handsomely, for in 1528 Lily's *Grammar* was made compulsory for all schools and was without a rival for the next 350 years. It remained in use at Eton until 1860.

Robert Large, Caxton's master, was as worthy a citizen of London as was Richard Whittington and the largesse he dispensed in his will on good works, both material and charitable, were in like measure to Whittington's bequests. He was typical of a new class that was emerging, a mercantile "middle class". Merchants, especially those in the wool trade, had become increasingly wealthy by comparison with the landed gentry and the old aristocracy. Some of them bought themselves social position by marrying above their

---

7. Walter Besant has left us a characteristically entertaining *Life* of Whittington (Chatto and Windus, London: 1881).

station. Sometimes kings sought their friendship – and financial assistance, from which often a knighthood would accrue, and sometimes an even higher honour. One of Edward IV's mistresses was the wife of a mercer, William Shore – who happened also to be a close friend of Caxton's.

With the wealth they acquired from trading in cloth some mercers aspired to become themselves members of the landed gentry by buying country estates. But in doing this they saw a commercial advantage too, as they thereby obtained control of wool growing, an essentially rural industry, at its source. This could explain how William Caxton whose father was a London mercer, came to be born in Kent. Robert Large was almost certainly one of these new country gentlemen, as can also be seen from his will, in which he leaves "to William Sampson my servant at my manor of Horham five marks". He left the same amount "for repairs in the nave of the church of Thakstede" and forty shillings "for repairs in the body of the church of Chawrey in the county of Essex".[8] That his origins were in this part of the country has already been suggested in our discussion earlier of the Little Wratting charters.

In London Robert Large dwelt in a style that befitted his wealth, in a fine mansion. It stood at the north-east corner of Old Jewry, which is still today so called because of the Jewish merchants who settled thereabouts at the beginning of the thirteenth century and built a synagogue in which to worship. But in 1262, in one of the pogroms that broke out regularly in the Middle Ages, many of the City Jews were massacred and those who survived were dispossessed of their synagogue.

In 1271 the building was given by Henry III to a community of mendicant friars, the Fratres de Penetentia, whose rule it would seem, was unusually liberal or even lax, as its members were allowed to marry and hold property. The only one of the customary monastic vows – chastity, poverty and obedience – to which they subscribed was obedience, and even this they do not appear to have observed very seriously. Perhaps because lay people found it hard to accept or condone such worldliness in a religious community the alms which were necessary for their support were less and

---

8. Blades 1877 pp. 152–55.

less forthcoming as time went on, and eventually the order was disbanded. In 1305 Edward I assigned the friary to Robert Fitzwalter, the first of a succession of City merchants to occupy it. A century or so later the house, now a handsome domestic building with but few of its earlier religious features remaining, became the home of Robert Large, and it was here that William Caxton came to live when became an apprentice.

The concept of apprenticeship had its beginnings in the ancient guilds, and though it had no legal sanctions until the passing of the Statute of Apprentices in 1562, it had become the recognised system of training for all skilled trades as early as the thirteenth century. By the time of Caxton it had developed into a code which was binding not only on the apprentice but on his master also. The statute of 1562, which remained in force until 1814, stipulated among other things that a uniform term of seven years must be served, though it is plain from entries in the Mercers' Account Books and the Plea and Memoranda Rolls that earlier on an apprenticeship could extend to ten or even fifteen years.

Before a man could set up in his own business he had to satisfy the wardens of his company that he had served an apprenticeship and was competent in his trade or craft. He could then on payment of a fee, which might be considerable, rank himself as a master and employ others and himself take on apprentices. If he lacked the neccessary funds to start up on his own account he became a journeyman hired by the day (from the French word *journée*). With the emergence of the capitalist merchants, of whom Robert Large is representative, the number of masters contracted and journeymen became more and more numerous in every trade. To better their conditions and obtain a living wage these skilled but poor craftsmen eventually organised their own guilds and sowed the seeds of modern trades unionism. As this situation developed the tendency was for affluent merchants to accept as apprentices only members of their own class or the sons of fellow liverymen and persons of financial standing.

The fact that William Caxton was indentured on the same date as his master's son, John Large, indicates again that despite his uncertain provenance Caxton's father must have been well-to-do. The acceptance of a lad as an apprentice was usually an undertaking to a personal friend, rather than merely a legal contract, and in effect placed the master *in loco parentis* towards his young charge. An apprentice was a pupil, not an employé or wage earner, and his master had very definite responsibilities towards him, accepting him as one of his family and providing him with board and lodging. A long time would pass before apprentices would suffer the degradations to which Oliver Twist was subjected, or be regarded as cheap labour recruited from the workhouses.

The household that William Caxton joined was a busy and sizable one. Apart from domestic servants something like twenty persons shared the roof: Alderman Large himself and his second wife, Johanna (and possibly a son of hers by a previous marriage, Richard Turnat); Large's own four sons, Robert, Thomas, Richard and John, whom his first wife, Elizabeth, had given him; his two daughters, Alice and Elizabeth; and eight apprentices. Among these Large's youngest son, John, whom we have already accounted for, is not included, but in order of seniority reckoned by their entry as recorded in the Mercers' books, the eight were Thomas Neche, Richard Bonefant, James Heton, Henry Onkmanton, Christopher Heton, John Harrowe, William Caxton and Robert Dedes.

Regarding the last named there is a little mystery. No mention of him occurs in the Mercers' records either of his entry or his issue, but in Robert Large's will which is dated 11 April 1441 he is referred to as "my apprentice" and is left the same sum as William Caxton received, namely twenty marks. Does the absence of his name from the Mercers' Account Books represent another instance of Robert Large's reluctance to pay his dues conscientiously, as Professor Blake suggested? It could be. But if the tone in general and the other provisions of his will are anything to go by, such an attitude would be quite uncharacteristic of the worthy alderman.

What is suggested by the fact that the two lads received the same amount under Large's will is that young Caxton and Robert Dedes were of much the same age, and it would be pleasant to think of them whiling away together what spare time was left to them after they had completed the daily tasks that their master demanded of them. The inclusion of the name of John Harrowe among Large's apprentices raises another interesting question. He is not mentioned in Large's will, but in the Mercers' records he is shown as issuing from Large's service in 1443. His father, also called John, was a contemporary of Robert Large in the Mercers' Company and is shown as having had an apprentice of the name of Richard Caxton who issued in 1447 (25 Hen. 6). Beyond this nothing certain is known of this Richard Caxton. Could he, as Besant speculates, have been a brother of the printer? He could quite well have been – and also the Richard Caxton who became a monk of Westminster Abbey in 1473, having tired of a wordly life in commerce. Blades contents himself with saying that "it is probable the two young Caxtons were of the same family". If they were, William Caxton would have had another companion for his leisure hours.

CHAPTER 3

Caxton's London

Like any newcomer the lad from Kent would lose no time in exploring the City. London had not yet become the sprawling metropolis of today and was still largely confined within the fortified wall with which the Romans had surrounded their Thames-side encampment, Londinium, and of which parts still remain – in the thoroughfare now called London Wall and in the churchyard of St Giles's, Cripplegate, as well as near Stationers' Hall and Amen Corner and on Tower Hill. It enclosed the area known even nowadays as "the City", which extended from the Tower in the east to Ludgate in the west, and was bounded by Holborn on the north and by the river on the south.

The most densely populated place in England, it had about 35,000 inhabitants, three times as many as the next largest city, York. Within the cramped walls there were no fewer than 136 churches, besides St Paul's Cathedral and thirteen monasteries. It is not surprising that by the beginning of the fifteenth century London was overspilling its original confines, mainly towards the west. All along the riverside, or the Strand as it is still called, houses and inns began to spring up, as far as the village of Charing, where there was the cross set up in memory of Edward I's queen, Eleanor, and the chapel of St Martin in the nearby fields, on the site of the present church. Beyond this was King Street leading to Westminster and Edward the Confessor's great abbey and ancient palace, where the youthful King Henry VI, who had succeeded to the throne as a baby roughly in the same year that Caxton was born, went through the motions of ruling the country – with the dubious assistance of his uncle, "good duke Humphrey" of Gloucester, who had been appointed his "protector", and the contentious and grasping Cardinal Beaufort, his illegitimate great-uncle.

Old London Bridge

Medieval London was a busy and prosperous port where ships from all the known world and especially the Mediterranean, from Baghdad and Damascus, Genoa and Venice, docked with cargoes of silks, satins, velvets, cloth of gold, damasks, furs, and exotic fruits and spices. These luxuries were paid for mainly with honest homespun cloth made from English wool, the trade in which had become the prerogative of the powerful Mercers' Company, of which young Caxton was now a cadet member. London was also the chief port of call for ships from the Mediterranean bound for Sluys, the harbour of Bruges, where later Caxton was to be the principal representative of the Merchant Adventurers.

Much of London's importance as an entrepôt was due to the fact that it was the lowest point at which the Thames was bridged. It was not until the middle of the eighteenth century that a second bridge was built at Westminster. Barges from many miles up river and the roads which converged on the bridge, brought wares from all parts of the country. Ships from the coast towns and from overseas could come up the broad tidal estuary to the Pool of London.

Constructed entirely of wood, old London Bridge had nineteen arches with a drawbridge between two of the piers to allow shipping through. Along each side of the bridge were houses and shops and in the very centre a chapel dedicated to St Thomas à Becket, in which Peter of Colechurch, the builder of the bridge, was buried in earth specially laid for the purpose. The bridge was regarded throughout the Middle Ages as a triumph of engineering and must have been one of the sights of London at which young Caxton, fresh from the country, gazed wide-eyed. At the same time a shiver must have run through him when he saw the heads of traitors stuck on the spikes over the fortified gate-houses at each end of the bridge. In 1438, the year he was registered as Robert Large's apprentice, five "risers", or rebels, from Tenterden in his native Kent paid for their crime in this way, and later in the same year seventy men from Rainham were convicted of treasonable assembly and of plotting to kill the king. Round this time Kent was the scene of a series of disturbances, caused mainly by groups of disaffected soldiers who had been disbanded after the death in 1435 of John duke of Bedford, another uncle of the young king, who when

A Medieval Banquet

the king's father, Henry V, the victor of Agincourt, died had been made "regent"of the territories that the English had conquered in France. To make matters worse England and the Continent had been struck by a famine and the demobilised soldiery were able to incite the starving country people.

Caxton himself recalls the catastrophe in the *Polychronicon*, the fourteenth century history to which he added from his pen an eighth volume called the *Liber ultimus* which brought the book up to nearly his own time. Caxton finished his writing in July 1482 and printed it soon afterwards. He relates: "also this yere was a greate derthe of corne in all Englond; for a bushel of whete was worth fourty pense in many places . . . wherefore Steven Brown, that time mayer of London, sent into Prussia and brought to London certayne shippes laden with rye, which eased and did much good to the people, for corne was so skarce in Englond that in some places poor people made them brede of fern rootes".

The mayor's providential action no doubt brought relief to the people of London, if not to the country in general. Merchants like Robert Large with their import–export connections would be well able to fend for themselves and their dependents so that William Caxton was unlikely to have gone hungry.

The table in Large's hall would be a movable construction of boards on trestles, round which the household would sit in order of precedence. As juniors Caxton and Robert Dedes would be at the lower end from their august master and his lady. A cloth of service-able linen covered the boards, on which were set knives and spoons – forks were a curiosity that came into use only in the reign of Elizabeth. What were fingers for, anyway? The cups and jugs were of wood or earthenware, except on special occasions when a man as wealthy as Robert Large would bring out his silver, or even gold, vessels.[1]

In the fifteenth century pewter – an alloy of the tin and lead which was widely mined in England – began to be used for mugs, and plates made of it largely replaced the wooden platters of earlier times. Earthenware plates were as yet unknown and meat was

---

1. In his will (v. Blades 1877 p. 155) Robert Large left "three cups with covers, from among my cups called standing cups of silver-gilt" to each of his daughters, Alice and Elizabeth.

usually placed on trenchers or thick slices of bread, which were afterwards given to the beggars who came to the kitchen door. Table manners fell far short of the ritualistic etiquette of later days and it was not thought amiss to fling the bones from which the diners had gnawed most of the meat on to the floor for the dogs. When the floor was covered straw or rushes were used. Carpets and woven rugs were regarded as an undesirable Continental fashion unworthy of an honest English home.

Breakfast for Caxton would be nothing more than a draught of ale and a piece of bread, but as early rising was the rule, dinner, the first of the two real meals of the day, was served at 10 or 11 in the forenoon and supper at 4 o'clock in the afternoon. Both were substantial repasts in a household such as Robert Large maintained. Medieval cookery was much more elaborate than is often supposed, and recipes that have survived from the fifteenth century were often quite complex and would make the mouth water even today. Spices which the City dry-salters imported from the Orient were used in a variety of sophisticated ways by well-to-do families.

A favourite dish was a sort of sausage which was made by pounding pork in a mortar with eggs and adding sugar, salt, raisins, currants, minced dates, powdered pepper and cloves, after which the mixture was boiled in a bladder and cut in slices. These were served with a sauce made of raisins, red wine, almond-milk coloured with saffron, pepper, cloves, cinnamon and ginger.

Caxton, like any other boy, would have a liking for sweets and no doubt his eyes lit up when there appeared on the table a sillibub – a concoction of wine or cider mixed with milk to form a curd, which was flavoured with fruit juices, whipped into a froth and then solidified with gelatine. Such dishes were for Christmas and other festivals. Everyday meals consisted of beef or mutton roasted on a spit or boiled, soups and stews thick with root vegetables, and bread and cheese. In Lent and on fast days, which included all Fridays, when no meat could be eaten, fish of all kinds were served, especially herrings, which abounded in the seas around England and if not eaten fresh could be salted or smoked to preserve them. Fresh water fish were eaten much more in those days than they are now. Fish ponds or "stew ponds" in the gardens of large houses were kept well stocked with eels and pike, which were served as a principal dish, the various recipes for which would be worth reviving.[2]

Except at banquets, when wine was served, ale was the universal drink and copious jugs of it were provided to wash down every mouthful. Ale was drunk in this country even before the Romans came. Beer, as distinct from ale, was introduced only in Caxton's time by Dutch settlers, of whom there were many in London and the eastern counties. Like ale it was a malted liquor, but was given its peculiar bitter taste by adding hops, the growing of which was to become almost a monopoly of Caxton's native county, Kent. Each inn in those days did its own brewing, and announced each new brew by putting out its "ale-stake", a pole with a bunch of leaves tied on the end, which was fixed over the door. In the narrow streets of London an ale-stake could be dangerous to horseriders, and by law was restricted to seven feet in length. The law also appointed "ale-conners", for not every brew was of the required quality, and it was the amiable duty of these officials to go and sample the new brew whenever the ale-stake was hoisted. The medieval tavern like the public-house of today was common ground for all kinds and conditions of men. William Langland, who had died only at the turn of the century, has left us, in *Piers Plowman*, a list of the regular customers of Betty the brewster.

Cis the sempstress sat on the bench,
Walt the gamekeeper and his wife – drunk;
Tom the tinker and two of his 'prentices,
Hick the hackneyman, Hogg the needler,
Clarice of Cock Lane and the parish clerk;
Parson Piers of Pray-to-God and Pernel the Flemish woman,
Dan the ditcher and a dozen more of them;
A fiddler, a ratter and a Cheapside scavenger,
A ropemaker, a lackey and Rose the retailer,
A watchman, a hermit and the Tyburn hangman,
Godfrey the garlic-seller and Griffin the Welshman . . .

There was nothing to prevent William Caxton from joining in such convivial gatherings, but as the terms of his indentures required him to be temperate he would not be a great frequenter of

2. This chapter owes much to L. F. Salzman's popular yet scholarly *English Life in the Middle Ages* (University Press, Oxford: 1926).

taverns even if he had the time. There were plenty of other things for him to see and do in his spare time. Robert Large's house in Old Jewry was situated almost at the very centre of the old city of London. Just round the corner in Canwicke Street was London Stone, which marked not only the centre of London but in a sense the centre of England. It was a milliarium or milestone which had been set up by the Romans nearly 1 500 years before to mark the point from which the British roads radiated, like a similar one in the Forum at Rome. It can still be seen today let into the south wall of St Swithin's Church in Cannon Street as it is now called. A few hundred yards away going west the gothic pile of old St Paul's Cathedral, built by the Normans, reared its great mass. In St Paul's churchyard, which was not used for burials, vendors had set up their permanent stalls or "stations" right up against the walls of the cathedral itself.

A custom in the Middle Ages and one which largely still persists, was for each trade to keep to its own street or district and often a trade would give its name to a place – Cornhill, for instance, and Fish Street. Most of the traders in St Paul's churchyard dealt in writing materials – quill pens, ink and ink-horns, parchment and paper. In the course of time these particular stallholders appropriated the name of 'stationer' for themselves exclusively. By 1403 they had formed their own trade guild, which in 1557 was incorporated as the Stationers' Company and given control of all printing in England, a move whereby Queen Mary hoped that the publishing of heretical writings would effectively be stamped out. When Caxton brought his press and type to England in 1476 he was not subject to any such restriction and he was not required, nor did he desire, to be a member of the stationers' guild, though the guild officers probably viewed with suspicion this new art which might threaten the livelihood of the scriveners and professional copiers of manuscripts. It is significant that at the end of the century when his successor, Wynkyn de Worde, moved the press to Fleet Street he considered it expedient to join the guild. The traditional association of stationers with St Paul's churchyard is preserved by their magnificent hall, which they built in adjacent Ludgate Hill.

In the same way the Mercers, when they were dealers mainly in small wares, had chosen as their market place the thoroughfare

A Medieval Marketplace, with the pillory where fraudulent traders would be pelted with their bad wares.

A Lollard being burned at the Stake.

known as Cheapside, which ran from St Paul's churchyard to Poultry. The latter was another street that took its name from its traders
– the poulterers who sold both laying hens and table birds. If Caxton was a squeamish lad he must have avoided this street, which
rang with the squawking of the fowls whose necks were wrung
when they were sold, to ensure that they were fresh for cooking.
Old Chepe was at the south end of Old Jewry where Robert Large
lived and in it was an Eleanor cross like the one at Charing. Round
this the humbler mercers who had not prospered to the same extent
as men like Large and had remained retailers, set up their stalls each
day. Later, in 1447, these former mercers were given their own
charter and became the Haberdashers' Company.

Also in Cheapside was a pillory, and Caxton would doubtless
join in deriding the miscreants who had their head and hands
locked in it. The pillory was the prescribed punishment for trading
offences among other misdemeanours, for in the Middle Ages there
was a customer protection code far more stringent than we have
today. Butchers who sold bad meat, bakers who made under-
weight loaves, and ale-wives who gave short measure all ended up
in the pillory.

The law could exact much grimmer penalties too. In his continuation to the *Polychronicon* Caxton tells how in 1439 Richard Wyche,
vicar of Deptford, went to the stake as a Lollard. A white-haired
ancient of eighty he obstinately clung to his beliefs, in spite of offers
of mercy if he would abjure them, and the Church authorities had
no option but to hand him over to the civil power for burning, as
provided for in the statute of 1401, *De haeretico comburendo*. The old
man was liked and respected by his parishioners and his case roused
a great deal of sympathy, so that double watches were mounted
throughout the capital on the night before his execution, in expec-
tation of a mob outburst. But nothing could save him. He was first
stripped of his office at St Paul's, and then led stumbling through
crowded streets to Tower Hill where he was roasted over a slow
fire, in the hope that he might still recant.

Caxton was probably not an onlooker as apprentices were not
free to come and go as they pleased, but that the occurrence affected
him deeply is plain from the account he gives. "This yere Sir
Richard Wiche, vicar of Hermettesworth was degraded of his

priesthood, at Powlys, and burnt at Tower Hill as an heretic on Saint Botolph's day; how well at his death he died a good Christian man, wherefore after his death much people came to the place where he had been burnt, and offered (prayers) and made a heap of stones, and set up a cross of tree, and held him for a saint, till the mayor and sheriffs, by commandment of the king and bishops destroyed it, and there made a dunghill." That the ecclesiastical establishment lost no time in removing the memorial cairn and desecrating the place with a dunghill is not surprising. They could not permit a martyr to be made of a man who had attacked the profligacy of the hierarchy, and less serious perhaps, had denied the efficacy of the mass and of prayers for the dead and sought to promote the pernicious doctrines of John Wycliffe, the renegade Yorkshire priest who, did they but know it, would later be hailed as the morning-star of the Reformation.

Among the City officials who were instructed to destroy the intended shrine was Robert Large, Caxton's master. On St Botolph's day, 17 June, when Richard Wyche died for his faith, Large was senior sheriff and mayor designate and as such would a few months later succeed Steven Brown in the mayoralty, having served the necessary term as a sheriff since 1430. Being a mercer he could expect the appointment fairly confidently, for membership of the Court of Common Hall, which had the right of choosing both sheriffs and mayor, was restricted to liverymen of the chartered companies. By weight of numbers the Mercers' Company could swamp these proceedings and in spite of widely expressed resentment on the part of other companies the Mercers provided on average more sheriffs and mayors than any two companies together. Moreover, the Mercers were wealthy, both corporately and individually, and they invariably occupied the mayoral office with dignity and subsidised it generously.

When one of their members was elected the inaugural ceremony and banquet in the Guildhall was lavish and unstinting. The "riding", or procession, of the new incumbent and his retinue through the City and on to Westminster to swear allegiance to the king, was even more spectacular than the Lord Mayor's Show of modern times. In the Mercers' Accounts there is an item dated 29 October 1439 for sixteen trumpets purchased for the "riding" of Robert

Large, mayor, at a cost of £5 6s 8d. It is also recorded that a number of liverymen who absented themselves from the festivities were fined.[3]

As a mere apprentice in the new mayor's household young Caxton would not attend the Guildhall banquet, though an unusually scrumptious feast for him and his like was no doubt laid on at the house in Old Jewry, after which he hurried off to join the crowds waiting to see the procession. This was literally a "riding", for everyone taking part was on horseback. It was only after 1711 when the mayor's horse threw him that coaches were used. In 1453, when incidentally Caxton himself was one of four liverymen fined for not attending, the mayoral progress to Westminster was made by river in state barges.

On such occasions the houses of the wealthier citizens were hung with brightly coloured buntings and silks. The shops would be closed, but the taverns and the stalls selling refreshments and sweetmeats did a brisk trade and the scene was still as William Langland had described it.

Cooks and their men were crying "Pies hot, all hot,
Good pork, good goose; come, come and dine".
Taverners told the same tale, "A drink of wine for nothing,
White wine, red wine, to wash the roast meat down".

In the side streets minstrels and balladmongers, itinerant players and mummers and puppeteers entertained the throng. If a pickpocket was caught red-handed he was not given to the watch; the belabouring he got from the crowd was reckoned as part of the day's fun. But the real spectacle of the day was the procession itself. First came the sixteen trumpeters, augmented by pipers and men beating tambourines and drums. Then came a bodyguard of pikemen and archers, some of the latter armed with the newfangled "crossbowes with a tourne" or windlass which Caxton mentions in *Fayts of Arms and Chivalry*. Next to appear was Robert Large, the new mayor, looking important and proud in the midst of the aldermen wearing scarlet robes and great hats of finest fur, their horses caparisoned with cloth of gold or silks and velvets. Stretching far behind were long files of riders representing the City com-

---

3. Blades 1877 pp. 9 and 146.

panies, with Large's fellow mercers naturally in the vanguard, all in
their distinctive liveries and on gaily trapped mounts. When finally
the pageant had passed, the cheering spectators would crowd into
the roadway and jostle their way along behind it. Some would
follow it all the way to Westminster, but others would soon fall out
and return to the taverns and sideshows. It was not often that they
got such a holiday.

On an ordinary day the common people, and apprentices also,
worked hard from dawn to dusk. As an apprentice Caxton would
not be given menial tasks about the house; there were servants to
do those. But he was kept fully occupied, learning his master's
trade in all its aspects. He would soon know how to distinguish the
various kinds and qualities of cloth – woollens such as frieze, rug,
kersey and cashmere; mixtures like linsey-kersey; linen from Ireland, cambric and fine lawn from France; silks, satins and samite;
figured brocades and damasks; velvets and velveteens. He also
helped check the stock, listing each delivery received and consignment out, a task he was probably given because he wrote a fair
hand, as can be seen from a manuscript in the Pepysian Library at
Magdalene College, Cambridge. He had in fact a very sound education by the standards of his time.

In the prologue to *The Life of Charles the Great*, which he translated from the French and published in December 1485, Caxton
wrote, rather smugly, "I am bounden to pray for my father's and
mother's souls, that in my youth set me to school, by which, by the
sufferance of God, I got my living – I hope truly". He was no
dedicated scholar however, either as a youth or later, as his somewhat pedestrian writings show. He regarded education as simply
something which would advance him in a commercial career, and
he was probably as unwilling a pupil as was Shakespeare's school-
boy. Though he would be made to continue his studies to some
extent while an apprentice – especially of subjects fitting for a
businessman – it is unlikely that he wasted any of his precious spare
time in the library that Richard Whittington had endowed in the
nearby Guildhall, or in poring over the illuminated manuscripts
which his master, like many other merchants, imported as a
sideline from Bruges. In any case these were intended for sale, not
for the idle enjoyment of either Robert Large or of members of his

household and their value would not be so great if they were soiled or finger-marked.

When his work was finished the young Caxton on lighter evenings in the summertime would sometimes accompany his friend Robert Dedes to the flat open area north of St Paul's called Smooth-fields, or Smithfield as it now is, for a game of football – not the orderly game that we know today, but a mêlée in which the two teams could be of any number of players, who for the most of the time were locked in one enormous scrummage in an effort to force the ball to one end of the pitch or the other. Here too were the butts at which he was required like all apprentices to practise regularly with the longbow, in order to be ready to turn out with the mayor's militia in the event of a riot or if the city should be attacked. Robert Large as a sheriff and prospective mayor would see to it that his charges put in their full stint of practice. In wintertime when darkness fell early, lamps consisting of a cotton wick floating in a bowl of oil and candles made by dipping twisted thread into melted tallow and building up layer on layer, gave only a feeble light. But this was sufficient to play card games or chess by, if the master of the house consented to his apprentices staying up for an hour or two.

Playing cards with much the same designs as our modern ones were introduced into England about the middle of the fourteenth century and by Caxton's time were widely popular. Another medieval game, not unlike backgammon, was "tables", which Chaucer mentions, and to which Edward IV became addicted in the indolent last years of his reign. But the most universally popular game of all was chess, so much so that "the meanest and simplest sort of people, yea, even the plain plowmen, were skilful at chess play". The game was of great antiquity; a version of it was known in pre-dynastic Egypt and over the succeeding centuries it spread across Europe acquiring new forms and new rules.

Caxton certainly took pleasure in the game, though the reason why he chose as the second book he printed *The Game and Play of the Chess*, which he translated in 1475 while still in Bruges, was probably because he considered it would find a ready sale. A second edition in fact was published in 1483 at Westminster, and although a completely new mode of the game had been introduced in 1480, the reprint was the same as the 1475 edition except that the dedication to the duke of Clarence, who had since been disgraced and done to death in the Tower, was omitted.

One good customer for the manuscripts that were imported from the Continent by Robert Large and other merchants was Humphrey duke of Gloucester, who in spite of his failings in other respects was an outstanding patron of painting and letters. He built up a large collection of manuscripts and classical texts which reveal an unsuspected side to the character of this otherwise unlikeable and truculent man. Many of them he donated to the University at Oxford to form the basis of its library. Though he was himself a latinist and inclined to favour the humanist writings which were beginning to find their way into England from Renaissance Italy, he also encouraged English vernacular writers, notably John Lydgate.

Lydgate, whose life overlapped that of Chaucer by some thirty years, was prolific in his production of narrative poems, songs, fables, allegories and pageants, and his longest poem *The Fall of Princes* was composed for Humphrey. His verses are far below the standard of Chaucer's work, but like Chaucer he was to be one of the authors whom Caxton selected for publication, for although he is little thought of nowadays he enjoyed a wide popularity in his own time and for several generations afterwards. It is due to Caxton that his *Temple of Glass*, which is in many ways an allegory in imitation of Chaucer's *House of Fame*, has been preserved. He was court poet in turn to Henry IV, Henry V and Henry VI, and Caxton must have heard some of the mumming plays and ballads which came from his pen. His authorship of the ballad *London Lickpenny* (or *Lackpenny*) is now disputed, but it conjures up one of the most vivid contemporary pictures of London life in Caxton's time, and contains the earliest record of the harmonious "cries" with which itinerant vendors offered their wares and which must have pleased Caxton's ears as he made his way about the streets.

The title of *The Fall of Princes* which Lydgate wrote for Duke Humphrey might be considered prophetic, as another addition that Caxton made to the *Polychronicon* gives reason to think. Caxton tells at unusual length of the trial and degradation of Humphrey's wife, a *cause célèbre* which stirred all London in 1441. Humphrey had been married before. His first wife was Jacqueline of Hainault who herself had earlier been married off by her grandfather, the duke of Burgundy, to John IV of Brabant, in an attempt to bring Brabant under Burgundian hegemony. This aim was thwarted when John was deposed; whereupon the Pope was persuaded to declare Jacqueline's marriage null and void. To the chagrin of the Burgundian ruler, who had expected that the Hainault lands would then revert to him, Jacqueline almost before her first marriage had been formally ended, accepted an offer of marriage from Humphrey.

Jacqueline's beauty and charm captivated the people of England when Humphrey brought her to London, but the ill-considered match came near to wrecking the alliance with Burgundy which had been of so much assistance in England's efforts to conquer France, as well as jeopardising the healthy state of trade which the Mercers and Merchant Adventurers had long enjoyed with the Burgundians in Flanders. Humphrey's elder brother John duke of Bedford, a diplomatist as well as a soldier, managed to save the situation for a time, but he need not have bothered unduly. The marriage of Humphrey and Jacqueline soon floundered. The duke was a notorious womaniser, and among his conquests was Eleanor Cobham, one of Jacqueline's ladies-in-waiting who was not only rated a beauty but also shared Humphrey's intellectual tastes. Before long she was sharing his bed, and when his marriage to Jacqueline was annulled and he finally married Eleanor, she had already borne him several children. For some reason she was as widely disliked as the "good duke", who was a skilled demagogue, was adored, and this was a weapon which Humphrey's enemies at court were able to use in their opposition to him. The Beaufort clique had long ago realised that when Henry V died of trench fever outside the walls of Paris, effectively there died with him any hope that a king of England would ever rule France.

With the death of John duke of Bedford in 1435 they would have made peace and withdrawn from France. But the reckless Humphrey, who on Bedford's death became heir presumptive and now claimed to be "sole protector", was assertive enough at meetings of the King's Council to get his own way and to keep the country in a state of belligerent patriotism. In rank and popular esteem Hum-

C

phrey was superior to the "peace party", but he was not even their equal in political guilefulness. They accused his duchess of practising sorcery and witchcraft. At first she was accused only of consulting Margery Jourdain the "Witch of Eye"[4], and of obtaining from her "medicines and drink" with which she "enforced the Duke of Gloucester to love her and after to wed her". Even in those days, when witchcraft was abhorred and feared, this would have been regarded merely as innocent superstitious nonsense. But at a second hearing a much more serious charge was alleged. It was said that she had procured a wax effigy of the king and had melted it before a fire with the object of causing the king to fail in health and die. The implication was that she was ambitious for her husband's advancement, and thereby her own, for if Henry should die Humphrey would succeed him, so there were plenty of people of all classes who would be ready to believe the charge.

The case against the duchess was strong, though quite plainly the two principal witnesses against her perjured themselves in a vain effort to escape the gallows. Humphrey realised only too well that his wife had in modern parlance been "framed" and that he himself was the target at which her accusers were aiming. Displaying a typical aptitude for self-preservation he callously abandoned her to her fate, shrewdly guessing that having succeeded in humiliating him through his duchess his opponents at court would not sentence her with the severity they meted out to the wretched Margery Jourdain, whose burning at the stake in Tothill Fields provided yet another entertainment for the mob. Even so Humphrey's duchess did not get off lightly. She was sentenced to life imprisonment and to walk through the streets of London on three successive days, barefooted, clad in a white sheet and carrying a lighted taper from the Tower to St Paul's, there to do penance in the presence of the mayor and sheriffs.

This sorry spectacle was staged on 13, 14 and 15 November 1441, and though to judge from the way in which he reports it William Caxton was an intrigued eye-witness, the mayor who supervised the proceedings at St Paul's was not his master, Robert Large, but Large's successor. Robert Large had died earlier that year.

---

4. Not Eye in Suffolk. Walter Besant, *Westminster* (London: 1895), p. 288 suggests that it was "Eye beside Westminster" or "Peter's Ey", now corrupted to Battersea – *ey* being a diminutive of *eyot*, an island.

CHAPTER 4

The Liveryman

What happened to William Caxton on the death of his master is as uncertain as just about everything else concerning him. He would not automatically be freed from his indentures. If an apprentice wished to continue his training in his chosen trade he might sometimes be transferred to another master on the death of his first, as there are instances in the Mercers' archives to show. But there is no record that this occurred in the case of Caxton.

On the death of a merchant his widow, if she so wished, was allowed to take over and run his business. In doing so she took on also all her husband's responsibilities including the care and instruction of his as yet unissued apprentices. Robert Large's widow appears to have done this, although by all accounts she was so distressed by her bereavement that at the interment of her deceased husband she publicly and solemnly swore: "I Johanna, that was sometime the wife of Robert Large, make mine avow to God and the high blissful Trinity, to our Lady Saint Mary, and to all the blissful company of Heaven, to live in chastity and cleanness of my body from this time forward as long as my life lasteth, and never to take other spouse but only Christ Jesu". At the same time the officiating priest vested her with a coarse brown veil, and placed on her finger a ring as token that she was thereafter wedded to Christ.

But though she thus took the veil it was not as a fully professed nun, but simply as an oblate, which meant that she could continue her secular life and go about everyday matters without constraint. To enable her to take on the management of the family business a degree of freedom was essential, as the four sons of Robert Large by his first wife had none of them reached their civic majority when their father died. John Large, the son whose apprenticeship was registered at the same time as Caxton's, appears to have predeceased his father, as he is not found mentioned in Large's will.[1]

As for the other three, Large's bequests to them were left in trust until they should "arrive at the age of twenty-four years". In the case of Thomas and Richard Large the bequests were put in "the safe custody and governance of the aforesaid Johanna my wife", and in the case of Robert Large junior in "the safe charge and governance of the aforesaid Thomas Staunton my brother". As there is no evidence of any blood-relationship between Staunton and Large, it can be assumed that Large simply meant that Thomas Staunton was his "brother-mercer", or if Staunton was the maiden name of Johanna Large, his "brother-in-law". Or conceivably Staunton could have been Large's half-brother. In the Mercers' accounts for 1432 he is referred to as "frere et Attone (attorney) de Robert Large."

The will provided that Thomas Staunton, Stephen Tychemerrsh and Arnulf Strete, mercer (father of Randolph Strete, another of Large's apprentices) should each receive appropriate remuneration if they would "undertake the executing of this my will and act in good diligence in this office". In Large's time the duties of trustees and executors were perhaps not so strictly prescribed as they are today, though the will did require Johanna Large, Stephen Tychemerrsh and Thomas Staunton to find "sufficient security in the chamber of Guildhall in the City of London according to the custom and usage of the said City". Apart from this however, men like Staunton and the others would doubtless be conscientious in seeing that their late friend's affairs and family did not run into difficulties, and Johanna Large would not be lacking for sound advice on how to keep the business on profitable lines.

In any case the worthy widow did not find herself unduly hampered by the vows she had taken and as time passed she found her loss less unbearable, so that as Blades wryly observes, her celibacy was not of long duration. Within a space of three years she had married for the third time. Her choice of a new husband showed she was as well able to take care of herself as of her family. He was as good a catch as Robert Large had been. By name John Gedney, a wealthy draper, he had been mayor in 1427 and had probably

---

1. Blades 1877 pp. 155-55 reprints a full translation of the will, except for one folio which has been lost.

known Large and been a visitor at the house in Old Jewry, for 1427 was the year in which Large was elected a warden of the Mercers' Company and began to move in influential City circles. But breaking her vows in this way was not to be viewed lightly. John Stow, the father of English antiquaries, recorded: "This Godnay in the yeare 1444 wedded the widdow of Robert Large late Maior, which widdow had taken the Mantell and ring, and the vow to live chast to God the terme of her life, for the breach whereof, the marriage done, they were troubled by the Church, and put to penance, both he and she."[2] Johanna Large did at least wait until she could discard some of the burden of running a business before remarrying. The year 1444 saw the issue of Richard Large from his apprenticeship with Geoffrey Fielding, as is noted in the Mercers' accounts.[3] He was therefore qualified to take up his inheritance and he could assist his mother more actively. The incidence of mortality in the Large family seems to have been unusually high, as Richard Large was the only one of the brothers to live to benefit under their father's will and accordingly the business came under his sole control.

As therefore the business remained in good hands after Robert Large's demise there is no reason to suppose that young Caxton's circumstances were affected to any great extent or that he did not remain at the house in Old Jewry, at least for the time being. He did not necessarily, however, complete his apprenticeship there nor is it necessary to assume that he was still living there when he issued. He may in fact have been in Bruges when he gained his freedom. This would explain why there is no mention of his issue in the Mercers' books. Caxton was to spend a great deal of his life in Flanders, of which Bruges was the commercial and civic capital, and he could well have been sent there while still in service with Robert Large's successors to round off his training.

Bruges was one of the most important centres through which trade with north-west Europe could be conducted, particularly in the commodities in which the Mercers dealt. Robert Large had extensive overseas connections and was doubtless in frequent

---

2. *A Survey of the Cities of London and Westminster.* The original text was edited by C. L. Kingsford, with notes and a *Life*, in 1908.

3. Blades 1877 p. 146 erroneously lists him as *entering* his apprenticeship in this year.

communication with Bruges. There is at least one note in the Mercers' archives of his having gone there personally in 1432, and in view of the incompleteness of these records this was probably not the only occasion. In the same way Flemish merchants would come to London, some of them staying at the house in Old Jewry, and it is possible that they condescendingly acknowledged the presence of young Caxton – one of Robert Large's most promising apprentices.

Generally, a man like Large would manage his business from his headquarters in London and leave the running of his overseas branches to his agents or representatives on the spot. Caxton could have been posted to Bruges as one of these while still an apprentice. This was not an uncommon practice. John Wheeler, "secretary" of the Merchant Adventurers wrote in 1601 in his book *A Treatise of Commerce*, which must be the earliest ever guide for businessmen: "The Merchant Adventurers send their yong men, sonnes, servants or apprentices, who for the most parte are Gentlemens sonnes, to the Marte Townes beyonde the seas, there to learne good facions and knowledge in trade." This was written much later than Caxton's time but could still apply retrospectively.

When Caxton himself first went to Bruges has been a matter for much speculation. Blades along with all the other biographers before him pursued the notion that he did so almost immediately following Robert Large's death. They took their stand on Caxton's statement in the prologue to the *Recuyell of the Historyes of Troye* to the effect that he finished his translation on 19 September 1471 and had then been for "the space of xxx yere for the most parte in the contres of Brabant, Flandres, Holand and Zeland". Taking his "xxx yere" at face value this could only mean that he had been abroad since 1441. But if he had it could only have been since *late* in 1441 as he would appear from his account of the occasion to have been in London in mid-November that year, when Lady Eleanor Cobham was made to do public penance. Apart from this, however, can we really accept that he had been abroad for exactly thirty years – no more and no less? Is it not likely that thirty is simply used as a round figure, as in other instances that can be found in medieval literature?

The whole exercise of trying to establish when Caxton actually left England has to date proved as fruitless as most other enquiries into his early life. One thing we know for certain is that he was already a person of some prominence in Bruges by the year 1450. Proof of this is the record, dated 2 January 1450, of a lawsuit heard before Roland de Vos and Guerard le Groote, two sheriffs of the town of Bruges, in which Caxton and another English merchant, John Selle, were sued for the not inconsiderable sum (in those days) of £110. It was not their own debt. Selle and Caxton had stood surety for a third Englishman, John Granton a stapler of Calais, who was alleged to owe the money to yet another English merchant, William Craes. This they must obviously have done some time before the date of the court hearing – from which we can conclude that Caxton was present in Bruges before 1450. William Craes had had Granton arrested because of the debt and Selle and Caxton had agreed to stand bail for him.

It is not an unfamiliar story. On being released Granton had skipped the country and Caxton and Selle were ordered by the court to honour the guarantee they had entered into.[4] Though all the parties in the case were English, the business between Craes and Stanton over which the dispute had arisen must have been transacted in Bruges, otherwise the court there would have had no jurisdiction in the matter. A more important conclusion that can be drawn is that Caxton was well known in Bruges and had built up strong connextions there, indicating that he had been there for a fairly extended period already. It does not mean however that he had settled permanently in Bruges, or that he ever did. He was what today would be described as an "expatriate". Even after he assumed the office of Governor of the English Nation in the Low Countries, his status would still be that of a "resident alien". Bruges would simply be the base of his commercial operations over there, and the distance between London and Bruges, or the rigours of travels in those days, were not so great as to preclude the possibility of his having journeyed between the two places quite frequently, as well as between Bruges and other places on the Continent in pursuit of business, whether on his own behalf or as the representative of others.

---

4.   Blades 1877 pp. 155–57 quotes the document in full, but misdates it 2 January 1449.

The misconception that Caxton left London in 1441 and stayed away for the whole of the thirty years is also based on the passage that we have already given from his prologue to the *Recuyell*. In this the phrase "for the most parte" is not intended to qualify "the space of xxx yere" which precedes it, but the words that follow it. What Caxton is really saying is that he was "for the most parte in the contres of Brabant, Flandres, Holand and Zeland". In other words he was not in the Low Countries continuously throughout these thirty years, though no doubt after 1462, when he succeeded William Obray as the Merchant Adventurers' chief representative and effectively became British consul, he would spend longer periods in Bruges than he had formerly.

His presence there would be necessary for him to deal with day to day transactions and in negotiations with the Flemish authorities, who for some years had been following an increasingly discriminatory policy against the English traders. But in his first years abroad, possibly for something like fifteen, though he was "for the most parte" in the Low Countries, he would no doubt need to return to England from time to time to report progress to his partners and discuss future dealings. This is a reasonable assumption, though actual documentary proof of his visits is lacking.

His presence in London in 1453 is as good as confirmed however by an entry in the Mercers' Account Book for that year, which records that William Caxton, Richard Burgh, Thomas Bryce, William Pratt and others were fined 3s 4d each for not attending the "riding" of the new mayor, Geoffrey Fielding -- who we will recall was the mercer to whom Richard Large, the only surviving son of Robert Large, had been apprenticed. It is unthinkable that he would have been so penalised unless he was actually in London at the time and his failure to turn out therefore without excuse.

It has already been surmised[5] that Caxton probably issued from his apprenticeship while in Bruges, where he had been sent to complete his training sometime after Robert Large died. Blades has apparently no misgivings in saying quite definitely that "Caxton issued out of his apprenticeship about 1446, and became a freeman

---

5. v.s. p. 69.

of his guild".[6] But rather inconsequentially he says on the page immediately following that his admission to the freedom was "shortly after he had issued from his apprenticeship" and "must have occurred before 1453, for in that year he made a journey from Bruges, accompanied by Richaert Burgh and Esmond Redeknape, when all three were admitted to the Livery of the Mercers' Company, a privilege to which the admission to the freedom was a necessary step". If, as we have noted earlier was Blades' view,[7] Caxton's apprenticeship "lasted but seven years", his assertion that Caxton issued from his apprenticeship in 1446 would be quite feasible, and it would give him time to make his way to a position in which he could stand surety for John Stanton in 1450. The only discrepancy appears to be that the lapse of time between Caxton's issue from apprenticeship and his taking livery seems to have been unduly long.

As we might almost ruefully expect, there is a problematical aspect to the manner in which his taking livery is recorded in the Mercers' accounts for 1453. In that year he appears to have transgressed the Company's rules in two respects. Not only was he among those who were fined for not being present at the new mayor's inauguration, as we have already mentioned, but it would seem that he failed to pay the fee due for his enrolment as a liveryman. When a member of the Company took livery he was required to pay a fee totalling twenty shillings, usually in three annual instalments of 6s 8d. In the list of new liverymen enrolled in 1453, one of them, a Henry Lytelton, is shown as paying the whole twenty shillings in a lump sum to cover the three years ("pur toutz iij Ans"). Sixteen others are shown as paying a first instalment of vjs viijd, among them Esmond Redeknape, Richard Burgh and William Caxton.

These last two names, however, have been crossed through with a pen, and an annotation alongside says "qz int' debitores copot", which in the curious shorthand of the clerk means "these are among the debtors at the end" – which indeed they are. The other fourteen are in due course shown as paying their second and third

---

6. Blades 1877 p. 16.
7. v.s. p. 40.

instalments of 6s 8d in 1454 and 1455, but oddly enough there is no subsequent mention of either Caxton or Burgh making any payment.

Blades' artless explanation is that "the usual fees on their taking up the livery seem to have been remitted", but there is no evidence to support his idea that the Mercers' Company ever excused an "overseas member", such as Caxton might have been considered, from paying his dues. Whatever the true explanation might be, the apparently lax attitude that Caxton displayed in 1453 towards the company's code of conduct did not hamper his advancement or impair his reputation. His eventual appointment to the powerful position of "Governor of the English Nation of Merchant Adventurers in the Low Countries", as in full it was grandly styled, proves that.

CHAPTER 5

The Venice of the North

The Bruges where Caxton became such a personage of note was renowned in the Middle Ages as the Venice of the North, a compliment which acknowledged not only its commercial importance but its pre-eminence as a cultural centre. From as far back as the tenth century its staple industry had been the cloth trade. To promote this trade regular markets and fairs were held on the Grand Place, where the Halles and their towering belfry, built in the thirteenth century, still stand as a reminder of the time when the city was the proud metropolis of north-west Europe, and when it outshone Paris and London, and almost rivalled Rome.

The cloth trade brought prosperity to Flanders generally, and in particular to Bruges, which at the peak of its career had a population of 100,000, and its artisans and traders formed themselves into as many as fifty different guilds and fraternities. But Bruges was much more than a manufacturing centre. Its elaborate canal system gave it easy access to Damme and Sluys, and the River Zwyn flowed into the North Sea, so that Bruges was able to trade directly with England and the Mediterranean maritime countries, not only to its own benefit but also on behalf of its neighbours in the hinterland.

Traders from all the known world flocked to this great mart town. Germans from the Hanse towns – Lubeck, Hamburg, Bremen, Danzig, Stettin – brought their wares overland to be exported from or exchanged in Bruges. On the Grand Place Venetians, Genoese, Florentines, Catalans, Portuguese, Parisians, English, Scots, offered goods of all descriptions, many of which were not intended for shipping to further destinations but for local consumption. Boom conditions, which it seemed would never end, had made the citizens and burghers of Bruges almost profligate in their pursuit of luxury. All that they could offer in return was the fine Flemish cloth for which they had for so many years been famed. To make this cloth they imported the raw material – wool – from England.

When eventually the English began turning their own wool into finished cloth in the reign of Edward III, who shrewdly persuaded about eighty families of Flemish weavers to leave their native country and subsidised them in settling in Kent, Caxton's birthplace, the effect on the general pattern of the trade was at first only slight. Before that time some 35,000 sacks of English wool a year had been sold to Flanders. Between 1400 and 1425 the figure fell to about 14,000 and by the middle of that century, when Caxton was actively engaged in the trade and based in Bruges, it was less than 10,000. It was then that Philip the Good, the Burgundian duke who ruled Flanders, came to recognise that England had become his country's principal rival in the international market for cloth.

Flanders had become a possession of Burgundy in 1384, when Louis de Mâle, count of Flanders, died. His only daughter, Margaret, had married in 1369 Philip the Bold, duke of Burgundy, brother of the French king Charles V, and as was the custom her husband assumed her inheritance. Philip the Bold, though a member of the house of Valois and owing fealty to Charles V, deliberately set out to establish himself as an independent sovereign. His son John the Fearless, who succeeded him in 1404, pursued the same aim. Only after the battle of Agincourt in 1415 and in face of the growing threat from the English king, Henry V, who still cherished the same preposterous ambition as his great-grandfather Edward III, namely to rule France, did the two factions draw together for joint defence. The rapprochement was short-lived, if indeed it was seriously intended by the French. At a meeting called in September 1419 at the bridge of Montereau to discuss the situation, one of the Dauphin's followers struck the Burgundian duke down and killed him. The cleft in the skull of John the Fearless was for long afterwards shown to those who visited his tomb as "the cleft through which the English entered France". John's son and successor, Philip the Good, immediately allied himself with Henry V.

Though Henry died in 1422, the English under his brother John

duke of Bedford, with the aid of the Burgundians continued steadily to overrun France and by 1428 were in possession of all the
northern provinces except Brittany. Only the exploits of Joan of
Arc gave the French a brief respite. Inspired by her the French army
rallied and drove off the English force which was besieging
Orleans, and for the space of a few months regained some of the
ground they had lost. Joan's capture on 23 May 1430 by Philip,
who callously and cynically sold her to the English, by whom she
was burned at the stake a week later in the market-place at Rouen,
enabled Bedford to take the offensive once more. By 1431 Bedford
thought he had a sufficiently strong hold on the country to bring
over his nephew Henry VI, a child of nine, and have him crowned
in Paris. The gesture proved futile, serving only to exasperate and
inflame the French. Philip himself had for some time been vacillat-
ory in his relations with England. The rash marriage that Humphrey duke of Gloucester had made with Jacqueline of Hainault had
already come near to alienating him.[1] In 1429 when for a time Joan
of Arc's star was in the ascendant he had in fact made overtures to
the newly crowned Charles VII, but drew back at the last moment.
His cordiality even towards Bedford, who in 1423 had sought to
cement the Anglo-Burgundian alliance by marrying Philip's sister
Anne, distinctly waned when after her death Bedford in 1432 married Jacquetta of Luxemburg.

In England support for Bedford's campaign in France was moral
rather than monetary, and in 1433 Bedford had to go to England in
person to plead for supplies. Philip realised, although Bedford faithful to Henry V's dream of an English king ruling France, did not,
that it was only a question of time before England lost the struggle.
Moreover, Philip saw that the eventual downfall of the English in
France could bring danger to himself. He urged the English to
parley with the French and arrive at some compromise partition of
the disputed territories. But at Arras in 1435 the Englsh demands
were so unrealistic that the conference ended with Philip separately
making a very satisfactory treaty with the French, which in effect
gave him all that he and his two forebears had ever sought – the
recognition of their suzerainty in the Low Countries, Luxemburg
and the territories of Burgundy proper. The English he left to

1. v.s. p. 65.

continue the war on their own, and this they foolishly did, even though Bedford had died two days before the conference.

It was under the rule of Philip the Good, who had so skilfully manipulated to his own advantage the long-standing antagonism between France and England, that Bruges reached the zenith of its fortunes, in a reign that lasted nearly fifty years. Though mentally and in his manner of life he was a Valois prince, his relations with France, because of the murder of his father, were never without a touch of mistrust. In 1420 he was still feeling vengeful enough to be one of the chief architects of the treaty of Troyes, whereby Henry V of England married Katherine of Valois and became ostensibly the heir to the French throne. He chose to make his home not in his native Burgundy and he set up his court in Bruges. Nevertheless he refused to bind himself personally to the English cause and would never accept the Order of the Garter. But he was careful to maintain the strong trade links which his Flemish subjects had forged with the English wool producers and for this reason he enjoyed their respect and loyalty. To demonstrate the importance he attached to this trade he founded a new order of chivalry in 1430 called the Order of the Golden Fleece.

The immediate effect, however, of Philip's treaty with France in 1435 was unfortunate. Flemish merchants in London were attacked and some murdered, and the bellicose Duke of Gloucester[2] raided the Flemish coast and blockaded the mouth of the Zwyn. Refusing to be provoked Philip forbade retaliatory action against the English traders in Bruges and made it clear that he wanted trade between the two countries to continue. The most he did to pacify his Flemish weavers was to impose a tariff on all English cloth imported into his realms. This he would probably have done anyway, for as we have noted previously the English had over the years been reducing the quantity of raw wool they sold to the Flemish weavers and had woven it themselves in an attempt to penetrate the market for finished cloth. All Europe was at the time engaged in a "trade war" and England was one of the leading contenders.

In spite of the prohibition on cloth, Bruges was still a good market for many other commodities, and if a merchant was willing

_____

2. v.s. p. 65.

to diversify his interests there were still handsome profits to be made. The Mercers certainly adopted this policy and it was in their twin role as Merchant Adventurers that mercers like Caxton were able to prosper. In any case there were other markets in the countries of "Brabant, Flandres, Holand and Zeland" where Caxton spent his "xxx yere", and unlike Bruges these had not adopted protectionism – places like Antwerp, where the importation of English cloth was free, and Ghent and Utrecht. As a merchant Caxton travelled widely throughout the Low Countries. As to what he dealt in, other than mercery, we have little documentary evidence, though Professor Blake has uncovered the odd fact that one of his sidelines was pewter.[3] There is also strong circumstantial evidence that like Robert Large before him he built up a trade in illuminated manuscripts, for which Bruges under the enlightened rule of Philip the Good was famous. Philip besides his other accomplishments was an impassioned bibliophile and left a collection of nearly nine hundred superb manuscripts, most of which can still be seen in the Royal Library in Brussels.[4] In the miniatures illustrating some of these the duke is shown visiting the studios of artists and scribes.

One scribe, David Aubert, is himself immortalised by having left behind a memoir of Duke Philip, written in 1457. "This renowned and virtuous prince has been accustomed, for many years past, to have ancient histories read to him daily. His library surpasses all others, for from his youth he has had in his service numerous translators, scholars, historians, and scribes in various countries, all diligently working, so that now there is not a prince in all Christendom who has so varied and so rich a library."

The production of manuscripts in Bruges was a thriving industry and on it was built a lucrative and specialised export trade with France, Italy, Germany, England and other countries. The English king of the time, Henry VI, bought manuscripts from Bruges, as also did John duke of Bedford and Humphrey duke of Gloucester.

---

3. N. F. Blake, *Two New Caxton Documents* (Notes and Queries, ccxii, 1967, pp. 86–87).

4. Patricia Carson, *The Fair Face of Flanders* (E. Story-Scientia, Ghent: 1969). Chapter III is a particularly evocative account of the Burgundian rulers of Flanders. Another fascinating picture of Burgundian culture is to be found in J. Huizinga, *The Waning of the Middle Ages*, translated by F. Hopman (Arnold, London: 1924).

Except for the sale of cloth in Bruges Philip placed no restrictions on the English traders there. In fact, because they observed his interdict obediently – at least they went through the motions of doing so – he tended increasingly in the years after the woeful events of 1435 to treat them with every show of favour. This was the general situation when Caxton first went on his overseas assignment, and in 1446 Philip appears to have expressed his earlier easy-going benevolence towards the English in some more definite manner. Though there is no evidence of a formal commercial treaty existing at the time, there are entries in the Mercers' accounts that suggest that Philip's duchess and her ladies were customers for gowns made in London.[5]

There is nothing to indicate how Caxton himself was faring in business at this time, or how he employed himself for the first few years he spent in Bruges. That he applied himself industriously to his trade and prospered we have already concluded from the fact that he eventually became Governor of the Merchant Adventurers – the highest position he could aim for, higher even than that of a warden of the Mercers' Company. It was from the Mercers' Company that the Company of Merchant Adventurers had hived off as an independent guild in 1296, though until 1526 the two organisations shared the same hall and recorded their proceedings in the same minute books. In 1344 they had on the instructions of Edward III established their principal staple, or overseas depôt, at Bruges. The nomination of the governor of the Adventurers there was until 1407 a royal prerogative, but in that year Henry IV granted them authority to elect their own candidate, a right which Henry VI (or his Council) renewed in 1444.

---

5. Blades 1877 pp. 29 and 146 cites four instances to support this.

PLATE I: The Langley Indulgence. The first piece of printing known to have come from Caxton's press at Westminster – a letter of indulgence issued by John Sant, Abbot of Abingdon to Henry Langley and his wife. The initial "J" of the Abbot's name can just be discerned at the top of the left-hand margin, where it has been drawn in by a scribe. The date of issue 13 December 1476, has also been written in by hand.

Edward IV   Elizabeth Woodville

Richard III   Henry VII

PLATE II: Caxton's Royal Patrons

CHAPTER 6

Our Man in Bruges

When Caxton first went to Bruges he almost certainly took up residence at the Domus Anglorum, the hostel or community house where most of the English traders lived, mainly for mutual protection. In their own country the English in the Middle Ages were notoriously xenophobic, a characteristic which possibly stemmed from their being an island people, and though such prejudice was not so strong among the inhabitants of Bruges, Ghent or Antwerp, where foreigners flocked from all parts of Europe, the English expatriates lived a life apart from the native Flemings in order to avoid any possibility of friction. Like the Easterlings from Germany and the Italians, who also had trading treaties with the Flemish merchants, they enjoyed certain rights and privileges granted and safeguarded by the Duke of Burgundy and the burghers of Bruges, but by the local people they would always be regarded with curiosity and often with an irrational hostility. So by day they went about their business circumspectly and with the coming of evening they closed the stout doors of the Domus Anglorum and kept off the streets and out of the taverns. Except that they took no religious vows their manner of life was almost monastic. Women were not admitted to the house on any pretext. All the residents were obliged to remain unmarried and anyone engaging in an outside liaison was liable to expulsion. This could explain why Caxton took a wife only late in life.

The rector of the Domus Anglorum was the Governor of the English Nation of Merchant Adventurers in the Low Countries. Though the Mercers' Company was historically the parent of the Company of Merchant Adventurers, the latter in the course of time became the statutory body to which the English government granted wide executive powers whereby they effectively controlled

81

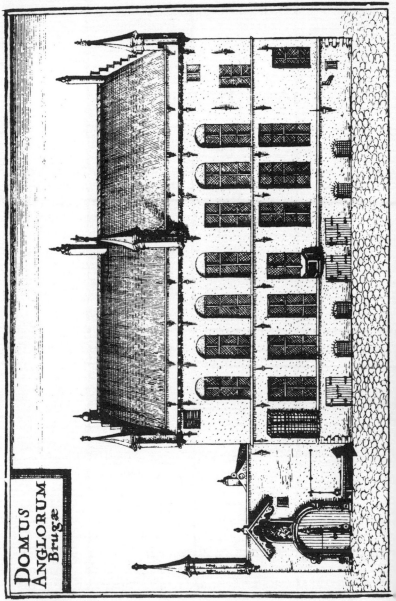

The *Domus Anglorum*, Bruges – Caxton's residence when Governor of the Merchant Adventurers.

all merchants both at home and abroad, and it was customary for any members of other companies who were engaged in foreign trade to seek affiliation with the Company of Merchant Adventurers and subject themselves to its regulations. Even so the Mercers, being the premier chartered company and the most numerous, were in a special relationship with the Merchant Adventurers and were able to dominate their proceedings. For the first hundred and fifty years of their existence the Adventurers shared the Mercers' hall, and in that period the majority of their Governors were mercers.

The influence that the Mercers wielded in the affairs of the ostensibly autonomous Adventurers is to be seen in the way in which they were able to bring to heel John Pickering, Caxton's successor as Governor. Pickering was alleged to have spoken disparagingly of the wardens of the Mercers' Company, and was summoned to appear before a court of the "Adventurers of the different Fellowships" in London. There he refused to "stand bare hed" and addressed the court "alle hawty and roiall". For this he was, on the insistence of the Mercers' Company, dismissed from his post and heavily fined. Only when he purged his contempt by humbly apologising on his knees was he reinstated.

It is not therefore surprising that the energetic Caxton, a mercer, should later be honoured with the governorship. It was an office that called for outstanding qualities of character. Its ideal incumbent had to be firm of manner, almost assertive, and possessed of an air of natural authority – yet for all that be courteous and conciliatory. He needed sound judgment and a shrewd business sense, combined with the ability not only to preserve the existing and acknowledged rights and privileges enjoyed by his fellow merchants, but also to seize every opportunity to extend them. To do this he had to be equally at ease with princes and with the commoners of the market-place.

The snobbish notion that "trade" is demeaning arose only in Victorian times, and the Governor of the English Nation was not only the agent of the merchants in London, but also of the king and various of his nobles. Henry VI's chief minister, the Duke of Suffolk, was not above procuring for himself a licence to export wool and made a fortune on the side. Henry's successor on the throne,

Edward IV, personally owned a sizable fleet of merchant ships which plied between London and Sluys. Another important function that the Governor was expected to perform was the gathering of intelligence on all manner of commercial matters, such as fluctuations in prices, market appraisals, forecasting the demand for various commodities (not only wool and cloth) and estimating their likely supply. Above all, as we shall see, he was the king's principal representative in negotiating trade treaties.

Such was the sort of man that Robert Large's young apprentice had grown into. But just when the governorship of the English Nation of Merchant Adventurers in the Low Countries devolved upon William Caxton is uncertain, as also are the circumstances leading to his appointment. Blades says that Caxton's immediate predecessor in office, William Obray (or Overey), would appear to have been the king's nominee. But as the Court of Adventurers had since 1407 enjoyed the right to elect their own candidate the king's part in his appointment was probably no more than a constitutional formality. Blades also says that Obray was appointed under a patent of Edward IV dated 16 April 1462 and implies that he held the post for only a few months, suggesting that he then died.[1] This is another of Blades's occasional slips, though it is of no great consequence.

There is evidence of Obray being in office in 1457, and the truth is that for years Obray used his position for personal gain and was eventually dismissed for peculation and corruption. One charge against him was that he had sought bribes from the merchants of Antwerp in turn for offering them some sort of trade preferences, though what these were to be are not exactly specified. His venalilty must have been considerable for him to be removed from office and must have gone far beyond the accepting of the customary perquisites that went with the job. The choice of Caxton to succeed him shows in what high regard Caxton had come to be held by that time, both among his colleagues in Bruges and by the Mercers and Merchant Adventurers in London. Caxton had now been a freeman of his guild for fifteen years or more and was a mature man of about forty. He could therefore be expected to bring to his high office experience and proved ability, and above all to

1.   Blades 1877 p. 19.

perform his duties honestly and conscientiously. He was the antithesis of Obray, his fellow-merchants considered – yet he was able, without incurring suspicion or giving rise to any doubts regarding his integrity, to accept gifts from various towns in the Low Countries that he visited.

There are several instances in the old account books of these towns of his being given a barrel of wine, sometimes two, but these gifts were openly made and were in no sense bribes or inducements. They were probably nothing more than the civic hospitality or entertainment that would normally be extended to an important visitor. The town records of Middelburg for 1470 have an entry to the effect that three quarts of wine were given to "Willem Caxstoen, meester van der Ingelsche nacie".[2] It seems to have been the practice almost everywhere for wine to be ceremonially presented to personages of note. In Bruges on 11 June 1469 the "ambassadors from England" received "trois pieces de vin", and in the same year Caxton is named in a list of notabilities who on 13 August shared the "Vins d'honneur" that it was the custom to distribute on great public occasions. Caxton received four "kans" of wine. Old records preserved in Utrecht mention his presence there in the years 1464, 1465 and 1467, and he appears to have enjoyed not only the town's largesse but also to have been given special clearance for the movement of his goods. There is not the slightest implication that any of the foregoing gifts were anything but expressions of respect.

They do indicate however, that the office of governor entailed considerable travel about the Low Countries. The position that William Caxton took over from the disgraced Obray was no sinecure and one thing that it required of him was to take up more or less full-time residence abroad. There is plenty of evidence that he travelled frequently to other towns on the Continent, but after 1462 there is no recorded instance of his making a journey to England. Though he would need to be in constant communication with the Court of Merchant Adventurers and the wardens of the Mercers' Company in London, as well as with the English government and the King's Council because of the consular duties that went with the post he now held, this seems to have been done by letter. An

2.   Crotch 1928 p. cxxxviii.

A dockside scene in fifteenth-century London

entry in the Mercers' accounts under "Foreign Expenses" in the second regnal year of Edward IV (1462) reads:

> Item for botehyre for to shewe to ye lordes of ye cousell the l're yt came from Caxton & ye felaship by yonde ye See . . . vj d

There are similar entries for later years. In these Caxton is specifically referred to or addressed as Governor. But in the entry just cited it is to be noted that the letter is "from Caxton & ye felaship". In another entry in the fourth year of Edward IV (1464) he is referred to simply as "Caxton ovir ye see". This suggests that for about two years following the exposure of William Obray Caxton was only a "caretaker" governor, though to all intents and purposes he was recognised both by London and Bruges as the senior English representative in Anglo-Flemish affairs. The first definite intimation that he had been confirmed in the post of governor is a minute of a meeting of the Court of Adventurers held at Mercers' Hall on 16 August 1465.

One of the responsibilities of the governor in Bruges was to ensure, through his "correctors" or inspectors, that all goods exported to England were of acceptable quality and of the contracted weight or measure. Three London merchants, William Redknape, William Hinde and John Sutton, had laid a complaint before the court that a consignment of cloth and lawn which they had received was defective. The court ruled that "a letter shal be made to Willm Caxton gouno^r by yonde the see"[3] The rebuke implied in this was no doubt purely formal, and in an oblique way acknowledged that Caxton could quite well be relied upon to see that cause for complaint would not arise in future.

The rights conferred on the Merchant Adventurers in 1407 by Henry IV and confirmed in 1444 by Henry VI were embodied in a new charter granted by Edward IV on 16 April 1462. By this the executive powers of their governor in Bruges were still further increased. He was expressly empowered to appoint at pleasure correctors and brokers to witness all bargains, as well as "folders and packers". Merchants were not allowed to pack their own goods and every parcel leaving the city was supposed to be sealed by the governor's officers, who were also required to be present at the

---

3.   Blades 1877 p. 20 gives the minute in full.

unpacking of goods newly arrived, in order to prevent any traffic in prohibited goods. On behalf of the governor these medieval preventive men levied a fee of 2d for every package exported or examined, and 1d was charged for the witnessing of any deed or transaction. As sometimes more than a hundred ships were at anchor in Sluys, the port of Bruges, Caxton's officers were kept busily occupied and the customs dues they collected amounted to no mean sum. Misappropriation of these funds could have been one of the temptations into which William Obray fell.

The need for this preventive service arose from the deterioration in relations between England and Flanders in years before Caxton took up his duties as governor. Ever since 1435, although Philip the Good had sought to encourage trade between the two countries, the Flemish weavers had opposed the importation of cloth from any other country – and in particular from England, which was not only threatening their home market but was also undercutting the prices that Flemish cloth had long commanded in Germany and other Continental markets. Mutual trade in other goods had continued more or less unabated, but by the time that Caxton became governor the loose concordat that had covered this had almost run its course. The situation was aggravated by the persistent endeavours of some English mercers to circumvent the regulations, in which they appear to have had official connivance.

The English merchants too resented the fact that Flemish cloth, which was of finer quality than that produced in England, could still be brought into this country and was in fact preferred by the fashion-conscious upper classes. At their insistence Edward IV's parliament of 1463 instituted duties on all foreign cloths, though these still left a loop-hole through which the well-to-do could continue to indulge their taste for finery. The Flemings retaliated with further imposts and the situation worsened, both commercially and politically – to young Edward's dismay.

He had shown himself to be a born general but he had yet to prove himself a wise ruler. Only now did he begin to realise that foreign trade and international politics are in many ways related. Though he had sat on the throne since 4 March 1461 his crown was by no means yet secure on his head. Henry VI and his queen Margaret of Anjou, and their infant son the Prince of Wales, were still at large in the North and capable of inciting rebellion. Even after their final defeat at Hexham in 1464 when Henry was captured and incarcerated in the Tower, Margaret was able to escape across the Channel to her native France. Her presence there constituted a greater danger to Edward. Louis XI, the new French king and her kinsman, not only gave her aid and comfort at his court; he promised her funds and troops to assist her in regaining the throne for her husband.

To counter these machinations Edward recognised more than ever that good relations would have to be restored with Philip, the Burgundian duke who ruled in Bruges, and who in spite of his defection from the English at Arras had maintained a state of armed truce with France.[4] Accordingly Edward set about repairing the damage that the restrictive practices of both the Flemish and the English merchants had jointly caused. What remained of any commercial treaty between Flanders and England was due in any case to expire on 1 November 1464. Cutting it rather fine Edward on 20 October 1464 appointed Sir William Whitehill and William Caxton to act as "oure true and accredited Ambassadors" to "our Cousin the Duke of Burgundy" with full power and authority to "make and conclude new arrangements".[5] The choice for this mission of a clever statesman and a successful merchant was a shrewd combination, and is again indicative of Caxton's stature. Nevertheless the most that Whitehill and his fellow envoy could achieve was to gain an extension of the existing agreement for just one year.

Philip, who could see through or was indifferent to Edward's political manoeuvrings and preferred to retain the support of his Flemish subjects, continued the ban on imports of English cloth. By dint of skilful diplomacy Whitehill and Caxton were able to obtain a promise that a "convencion of the lordes" to discuss the situation further would be held at St Omer on 1 October 1465. For some reason this meeting did not take place, and on 17 October 1465 the four wardens of the Mercers' Company wrote anxiously to Caxton reminding him that the renewal period would itself expire "the ffirst day of Novembre next comyng". Their letter was

4. v.s. p. 77.

5. Rymer's *Foedera* (London: 1710) Vol XI, p. 536. Blades 1877 pp. 162–163 quotes the commission in full (in translation).

to no avail, and Caxton, who no longer had the assistance of Whitehill, was unable to do anything to resolve the situation. English cloth, which represented the major element in English exports, was still excluded from Philip's dominions. In reprisal the Mercers saw to it that a large range of Flemish goods were banned in England. The result was that merchants – both English and Flemish – who dealt in other goods than cloth took to smuggling on a still more serious scale.

At this stage Warwick the "Kingmaker" intervened. He had motives of his own for entering the dispute. It was he more than anyone who had been instrumental in putting his cousin Edward IV on the throne and for the first years of Edward's reign he regarded himself as "everything in this kingdom". Edward IV was, so he thought, his puppet. For dealing with any possible danger from the indomitable and vengeful Margaret of Anjou in her refuge in France Warwick had ideas of his own. He advocated détente with France. To gain this he was ready to sacrifice trade with Flanders and he wrote to Caxton ordering him to ensure that English traders abstained from dealing in any goods that had been declared contraband by Act of Parliament. Caxton, himself not a man to be easily abashed, in a letter dated 27 May 1466 sent a copy of Warwick's order to the Court of Adventurers in London and to the mayor asking advice as to how he should treat Warwick's instructions. Again the power of the Mercers' Company was demonstrated.

A meeting of the full Court of Adventurers was convened immediately Caxton's letter was received on 3 June and the very next day a reply was despatched telling him that he was to "consider and fulfill th'entent made by acte of p'lement and the speciall desire of oure forsaid lorde". Furthermore the court said they were "willyng in no kynde the said acte to be broken nor hurte by non of oure felyshipp" and that anyone infringing it should "do correcion". It was the Mercers' interests that were at stake, and significantly though the letter was addressed to "Willm Caxton Guno^r de la nac' deng^s", the four signatories were the "Custoses of the mercery & thaventerers of the same".[6]

---

6. Blades gives verbatim copies of both these letters in *The Life and Typography of William Caxton* (1861–63) Vol I, pp. 90–92.

In view of this continuation of the embargo by both the English and the Flemish authorities it was now necessary for Caxton's preventive men to be more than ever vigilant. As for the injunction that offenders should "do correcion", under the charter of 1462 Caxton or his personally appointed deputies had almost viceregal jurisdiction – not only to arbitrate in all disputes between English residents in the Low Countries, but in cases of misdemeanour or felony to pass sentence in a court composed of himself as governor and twelve "justiciers" – chosen by the "common merchants and mariners" but subject to his approval – to counsel and advise him. To back up the judgments of the court there were six serjeants "to do the executions and arrests of the said court".

By nature Caxton was not a political animal; he was first and foremost a merchant. But whether he liked it or not, as Governor of the English Nation of Merchant Adventurers he found himself inextricably involved in the political intrigues of his time. The implications of the rivalry between the houses of York and Lancaster at home were not lost on him and neither were those of the rivalry between the houses of Valois and Burgundy on the Continent. As a merchant he would favour the party in England which was more likely to succeed in restoring a prosperous state of trade with Flanders, and it was for this reason that he viewed Warwick's interference in the situation with misgiving and was bold enough, though he did it discreetly, to indicate this in his letter of 27 May 1466.

Despite his immense executive authority there was little he could do to alter the situation while Philip the Good in Bruges persisted in his policy of conciliating the Flemish merchants and while Warwick held the reins of power in England. Though Warwick's influence over Edward IV was already waning, and Philip, now nearing his seventieth year, in 1465 began more and more to delegate responsibility to his son, matters were to remain in the frustrating and unsatisfactory state that we have described until Philip died in 1467 and Charles the Bold succeeded him.

CHAPTER 7

Meanwhile back in England

When Caxton, still bound apprentice, went to Bruges, he would be more taken up with what was happening in that city rather than in England or in France. But events at home, certainly major ones, must have impinged upon his notice and remained vividly in his memory for him to have been able to recall them when later he set about writing his continuation to the *Polychronicon* and when making his additions to *The Chronicles of England*. What then was happening back in England while Caxton was for thirty years mostly abroad? Truly the country was in a sorry condition.

In 1442 there were already rumours that the king was feeble-minded, and the feuding among his uncles during his long minority produced opportunities for self-aggrandisement which magnates outside the royal circle were quick to exploit. Typical of these was William de la Pole, earl of Suffolk. He is the prime example of the new capitalist mercantile class that had emerged.[1] His great-grandfather had been a Hull merchant and the Beauforts never missed an opportunity to remind him of it, though he was in a remote way one of them. He had married Alice Chaucer, grand-daughter of the poet and of Philippa Swynford – a sister of Catherine Swynford, John of Gaunt's mistress and mother of the illegimate Beaufort brood. In spite of the Beauforts and of Humphrey duke of Gloucester, Suffolk subtly managed to win the confidence of the adolescent Henry VI and obtained almost complete political control in both home and foreign affairs. Abroad, since 1435, when Philip of Burgundy made a separate peace with Charles VII and when John duke of Bedford died, the English campaign in France had gone from bad to worse, despite the jingoism of Bedford's brother Gloucester.

---

1. v.s. p. 83.

Town by town the French recaptured the territory they had lost. By 1444 the war was going so badly that the "peace party" headed by the Beauforts and Suffolk, were so anxious to disengage from further hostilities that they manipulated the pious and pliant Henry, now twenty-two years old, into agreeing to a marriage with a French princess, Margaret of Anjou, niece of Charles VII. John Lydgate as appointed court poet and poet laureate in almost our modern sense, wrote a somewhat laboured epithalamion for the occasion. It was Suffolk who went to France to escort Margaret to England.

Margaret was only sixteen, but already she possessed the passion and resolute spirit that was to win for her the unflattering soubriquet "she-wolf of France". Though beautiful she was unpopular in England right from the start, mainly because Humphrey of Gloucester was able to direct towards her the mob's resentment at what they saw as capitulation to the French. It is true that she personally persuaded Henry to order the surrender to Charles of the whole county of Maine, one of the few territories where England had still a foothold. The truce that his policy of appeasement bought did not last long. Charles VII had set his heart on full and final repossession of all lands that the usurping English still held. Though the war-mongering Humphrey died, in suspicious circumstances, in February 1447, his supporters had enough influence to pursue a policy of continuing the English presence in France and even of extending it.

A raid into Brittany from English-occupied Normandy was regarded by Charles as breaking the truce, and he declared war again in July 1449. Within a year the English had been driven out of Normandy. Charles had not wasted the two years of truce, but had spent them in reorganising and re-equipping his army with the new artillery, which made it far superior in fire power to the logistics favoured by the English commanders – a combination of archers and men-at-arms – which though it had gloriously won the day at Crecy and Agincourt was now plainly outmoded. The blame for the disaster in Normandy was laid on William de la Pole, now duke of Somerset, whom the Beauforts were able and happy to abandon to the role of scapegoat, as he had made enemies on all sides by his personal greed and rapacious administration – though the command in Normandy had been held by Edmund Beaufort, duke of Somerset.

Suffolk was impeached, but the gentle and ever-forgiving Henry would do no more than order him into five years exile. On his way across the Channel in a ship of Henry's on 2 May 1450 Suffolk was clumsily and barbarously beheaded by the mutinous crew. Mutiny and rebellion were in the air everywhere in England. Just three weeks after the lynching of Suffolk the "commons of Kent", the county that Caxton hailed from, rose under Jack Cade. Henry, for all his pacificism, was never a coward. On 11 June he faced up to the rebels at Blackheath and got them to disperse.

The great wave of disaffection at the grass roots that culminated in Cade's rebellion was quickly followed by a greater challenge to the corrupt government – and as it transpired to the future of Henry himself. This came from Richard duke of York, who having contributed to the downfall of Suffolk, now turned his attention to Suffolk's successor as the king's favourite counsellor – Somerset, who since the death of his wily uncle Cardinal Beaufort, had been chief of the Beaufort clan. With the death of Humphrey duke of Gloucester, York had become heir presumptive to the throne as the only direct descendant of Edward III through a legitimate line.

The first Beauforts though legitimatised by Richard II had been excluded from the succession by a decree of Henry IV. But after a lapse of two generations Edmund Beaufort, now entrenched in the King's Council and in Henry VI's personal esteem, hoped that the prenuptial birth of his forebears might be overlooked and that he might yet be recognised as the Lancastrian heir if Henry should continue childless. By skilful scheming that came naturally to a Beaufort he was able, he thought, to clear the way for himself by persuading Henry to appoint York to the lieutenancy of Ireland for the unusually long term of ten years. But in the September following the Kentish rising York returned without permission from his virtual exile, declaredly to deny the persistent imputations that he had secretly backed Jack Cade. Certainly one of the so-called "complaints of the commons of Kent" had been that York should not be excluded from his rightful place at court and among the king's advisers, and Cade had asserted himself to be in reality John Mortimer and a kinsman of York's. The true identity of the rebel commander has remained an unsolved mystery and the truth of York's implication in the rebellion has never been established either way.

Subsequent events were to prove York to be as consummate a schemer and as selfishly motivated as ever Somerset was. He shamelessly curried favour with the people and when a rabble of ex-soldiers attacked Somerset's lodgings at Blackfriars, York saved him from violence, but then took him by barge to the Tower, where he put him into "protective custody". Genuinely or not, York took up the role of reformer of the administration, and though he attracted little support from the lords his following among the commons was strong and they elected his chamberlain as their speaker. In spite of this a bill they presented asking Henry to recognise York as his heir was thrown out and parliament was dissolved in May 1451.

Henry's queen, Margaret, though still only twenty-one had become a power to be respected in the inner circle of the court and naturally had the ear of the king. She obtained the release of Somerset and through him became effectually the leader of the royal party. The rivalry between Somerset and York grew into open emnity. In 1452 York attempted by means of an armed coup to take control of the administration. He marched on London with an army, but when the city authorities refused to open the gates to him he protested his loyalty to the king himself and took up camp at Dartford, from where he demanded that Somerset should be dismissed from office and put on trial for his military failures in Normandy. He was tricked into thinking that his wishes were to be met, but when he went to face the king he found Somerset in his usual place beside Henry, and it was York, not Somerset, who found himself under arrest. Though York's actions had been undoubtedly treasonable, Henry showed his customary leniency, recognising that the real issue was the deep animosity and jealousy that existed between the two peers. The humiliated York was allowed to go free after solemnly affirming his loyalty to Henry in a well staged ceremony at St Paul's Cathedral.

The next year, 1453, the year Caxton was in London to take livery, two almost catastrophic events turned the situation in York's favour again. And in the royal household what is often termed a "happy event" occurred which was to bedevil the contest for the succession. In July 1453 the French artillery just about wiped out the last English army in Gascony at the battle of Castillon. This alone would probably have been sufficient to discredit Somerset for good, but his downfall was postponed by a misfortune at home.

Early in August the king had a complete mental breakdown which was to leave him incapable of speech or movement for nearly eighteen months. York immediately insisted that he, and he alone, had any right to act as regent. His position as heir presumptive, however, was over when in October the queen bore a son. In view of Henry's known fastidiousness in matters of sex and that eight years had passed since his marriage, there were slanderous suggestions that Margaret had not been faithful to him.[2] York himself did not join in these and almost ostentatiously recognised the child as heir to the throne, but Margaret's long-standing mistrust of the duke was not allayed. York however was readmitted to the council and to some extent exercised the power he had long sought.

But after Christmas 1454, when Henry began to show signs of recovery, Margaret persuaded him to dismiss York and reinstate Somerset. Still far from well again, Henry was soon under the thumb of his wife once more, and apparently accepting the situation York and his supporters retired to their strongholds in the North, but not for long. In May 1455 York with an army set out for London. At St Albans more by chance than design he met Margaret and Somerset, who were on their way with Henry to hold a Great Council at Leicester. The royal party had an army with them for protection, and confronted York's troops. Two front attacks by York failed, but his doughty lieutenant Richard Neville earl of Warwick, made a surprise attack from the side streets, in which Somerset was killed. Henry himself was slightly wounded in the neck by an arrow, but Margaret was able to escape.[3]

After the first battle of St Albans (22 May 1455) Henry VI was

2. It was even rumoured that Somerset was the father of Margaret's child, and Warwick openly said that the father was a strolling player. According to a story that circulated on the Continent, when Henry himself was shown the baby he exclaimed that it must be the child of the Holy Ghost.

3. William Seymour, *Battles in Britain* (Sidgwick and Jackson, London: 1975), Vol I (1066–1547), Chapter 7.

virtually a house prisoner, and Richard of York was acknowledged as *de facto* regent. But Margaret of Anjou, "a great and strong laboured woman"[4] and the real power behind the throne, patiently nursed her resentment and plotted revenge, not only on Richard but also on his principal supporters, the two Nevilles, Salisbury and his son Warwick. In November 1458 Warwick was involved in a fracas between his retinue and the guard of the royal household, in which he came near to being murdered. The queen blamed Warwick and demanded his arrest,but he forestalled her by taking off to Calais, of which he had been appointed Captain in 1450, and though he was deprived of the captaincy in his absence he defiantly retained his command of the garrison there. The old court party, still smarting from their humiliation at St Albans, suspected – with good reason as it later proved – that York's hope was to seize the crown rather than be content with the role of regent. The following September Warwick returned, bringing with him some of the Calais garrison to join Richard, with whom Salisbury had already linked up at Ludlow. Margaret was able to rally an army and her forces managed to defeat the Yorkists, largely owing to the desertion of most of the troops that Warwick had brought from Calais. York fled to Ireland and the Nevilles to Calais, taking Richard's son and heir, Edward earl of March, with them.

It was from here that in January 1460 John Denham, a Yorkist captain, led a raiding party on Sandwich and captured Lord Rivers and his son Anthony Woodville. We shall hear much more of Anthony Woodville, for he was later to be William Caxton's friend and patron, and translator of the first book ever printed on English soil. The Woodvilles as they are usually called, though in medieval records they appear variously as Wydville, Wydvile or Wodeville, had come up in the world. Richard Woodville, Lord Rivers, was the son of a humble knight and was himself knighted for his part in the French campaigns of John duke of Bedford, Henry V's brother who became "regent" of France when Henry died of trench fever in 1422 at the early age of thirty-two. When Bedford himself died in 1435 Woodville married his commander's widow, Jacquetta of Luxembourg. For this the two had to seek pardon for marrying

---

4.   J. Gairdner, *The Paston Letters: 1422–1509* (Chatto and Windus, London: 1904), Vol I, 275.

without the king's permission and Woodville was fined for his presumption. Although the court "establishment" regarded him as an upstart he later found favour with Henry, perhaps because Jacquetta was a cousin of the queen. It was not long before he was created Baron Rivers and appointed Treasurer and High Constable of England.

Rivers had been sent to Sandwich to keep an eye open for any preparations that might be made by Warwick to mount an invasion from Calais. When the captive Woodvilles were taken before the three noble refugees in Calais the ageing Salisbury angrily rebuked Rivers "that he should be so rude to call him and these other lords traitors, for they shall be found the king's true liege men". Warwick and March "rated him in like wise".[5] And the king's true liege men they were indeed – until events made them otherwise. For when on 10 July 1460 Warwick, Salisbury and Edward re-entered the country, routed the king's army at Northampton and took him prisoner again, they treated him with every courtesy and show of respect, although the lords, knights and squires who had fought with him and had survived the battle were killed out of hand.

It is one of the many ironies of history that Edward and Anthony Woodville, now in opposite camps, were to become the closest and most affectionate of friends. When they faced each other at Calais they were both of the same age, youths of seventeen – though that was a mature age in those fast-moving days. Both were handsome and both were to show themselves brave. Edward was six feet four inches tall, slim and wiry, with broad shoulders, blue eyes, fair hair and he had a ready smile. But Anthony had a more kind and gentle nature and was to prove the more knightly of the two and the more cultivated and sensitive – characteristics which Edward, in spite of his coarser fibre, came to admire in his friend. Anthony Woodville was Chaucer's "very perfit gentle knight".

York himself did not venture back from Ireland until two months after the battle of Northampton. But once in London, to the surprise of Salisbury and Warwick and possibly of his son, he immediately announced that he had a better right to the throne than Henry. He was not only a paternal great-grandson of Edward III, through Edmund of York, Edward III's fifth son, but was also

---

5.   Gairdner, *The Paston Letters*, Vol I, 346.

descended on the distaff side from Edward's "third goten son" Lionel, through his mother, Anne Mortimer.

The gentle-natured Henry had always had a guilt complex about the manner in which his grandfather Henry Bolingbroke had dethroned and murdered his own cousin, Richard II, Edward III's undoubted legal heir, and he mildly asked his assembled lords to decide on the merits of York's claim. Henry, for all his fecklessness and susceptibility to place-seekers, was not disliked by the lords at large and they came up with a compromise solution – which like most compromises was to prove no solution at all. While they declared that York had the more proper title to the throne, they were reluctant to unseat Henry. Instead they suggested that Henry should remain king for the rest of his life and that York should succeed when Henry died. As York was older than Henry by ten years this might have seemed to them a smart move and they were perhaps surprised, or even puzzled, when York agreed to it with apparent readiness. York was simply biding his time with the best grace he could and would probably have found a way of disowning the arrangement when a favourable opportunity arose.

In the event he was forestalled by the redoubtable Queen Margaret. The rights of her son, the seven-years old Prince of Wales, had been completely ignored in the compromise reached by the lords. To challenge it she got together an army, oddly enough in York's own county. In December 1460 York, accompanied by his second son, Edmund earl of Rutland, and the faithful Salisbury, hurriedly went north to confront her, leaving Edward earl of March to follow with reinforcements. Before Edward could do so the battle of Wakefield was joined on 30 December. Vastly outnumbered, York, still only forty-one, was defeated and slain along with young Rutland. The sixty-years old Salisbury was led away to nearby Pontefract Castle and ignominiously beheaded.

According to Professor Blake another casualty of the battle of Wakefield was John Harrowe, who is probably to be identified with the former fellow-apprentice of Caxton in the service of Robert Large.[6] Evidently less circumspect than Caxton, Harrowe was among those taken at Wakefield and beheaded. Professor Blake cites no sources for this information, but if it is correct Harrowe

---

6. N. F. Blake, *Caxton and his World*, p. 40.

must have been of some prominence in the Yorkist cause, as it was the custom to execute only prisoners of rank – lords, knights and squires – and to allow the ordinary soldiery to go free after disarming them. York's heir, Edward, might have met his death also at Wakefield if he had arrived in time for the battle. As it was, he lived to fight another day.

Four months after the battle of Wakefield many of the same lords who had been unwilling to depose Henry in favour of Richard of York now agreed that Edward should have the throne. In their view Margaret's action had acquitted them of their undertaking to exclude York from the succession until such time as her husband died, and with York now dead they declared, still reluctantly, that his son should immediately take the throne as the rightful king of England, and that the usurping Lancastrians should be reduced to their proper station.

Salisbury's long-standing commitment to the Yorkist cause can perhaps largely be explained as stemming from the fact that Richard of York was his brother-in-law, having married Cecily Neville, Salisbury's youngest sister. The large family of Nevilles (Salisbury's fourteen brothers and sisters and his own four sons) could therefore have expected to prosper if York's kingly aspirations had been fulfilled. For the same reason Salisbury's son, Richard earl of Warwick, on York's death at Wakefield set himself to put his cousin, York's son, on the throne.

He was personally ambitious and expected that as Edward was still only nineteen, he would himself become the executive head of state. If he thought so he underestimated the strong-willed, even wilful, Edward. In any case, before he could become 'Kingmaker', he had to ensure his own safety, for if the Lancastrians were to consolidate the advantage they had gained at Wakefield he could expect to meet the same fate as his father. And this nearly happened. In February 1461, two months after the battle of Wakefield, Queen Margaret marched south and in the second battle of St Albans thoroughly outfought Warwick, so revenging the defeat that he had inflicted on her at the same place six years before. Warwick in spite of his reputation was not a great soldier; he was more a political opportunist. With what remained of his army he managed to escape.

Again Henry VI proved to be his own worst enemy. He pleaded with Margaret not to take her battle-crazed forces on to London, where they might go on the rampage. With a deference quite uncharacteristic of her she held back, and while she hesitated Warwick joined up with Edward, who had recruited a new army in the Welsh marches, and together they entered London. On 4 March 1461 Edward was acclaimed king in Westminster Hall. But wasting no time on celebrations, Edward and Warwick set off in pursuit of Margaret, who retreated north. On 29 March they caught up with her at Towton, near Tadcaster, and in the bloodiest battle of the war, fought out in a fierce snow-storm, routed her utterly.

With Henry and their eight year old son and a few surviving loyal nobles, she fled to Scotland, and for the next three years organised resistance. Louis XI of France, who was related to Henry and to her (he was a grandson of the mad Charles VI and great-nephew of Charles' daughter, Katherine, Henry's mother, who had been married off to Henry's father after his victory at Agincourt), gave her financial assistance and also sent her a small number of French troops. With these and some Scots levies she harried the north of England, capturing Yorkist strongholds like Bamburgh, Alnwick and Dunstanburgh, but subsequently having to evacuate them again on the approach of superior Yorkist forces.

Edward, finally exasperated, himself took a massive army north. At Hexham, in the spring of 1464 Margaret's motley army was finally smashed. With the young Prince of Wales she managed to escape to France. That was not, however, the last that would be heard of her. The hapless Henry VI, who had never had a stomach for violence, went into hiding in Lancashire. Rejected by his one-time friends he wandered in disguise from shelter to shelter, until the summer of 1465, when Edward's men captured him near Clitheroe. Professor Blake, citing two unspecified chronicles, credits the arrest of Henry to another London mercer, William Cantelowe, who he says "was made a Knight of the Bath at Edward's coronation, which he had no doubt helped to bring about", and dates the event as occurring in 1467.[7] According to Hearne's Fragment (Chapter 9), "King Harry was taken in a wood by one William Cantlow" whose trade or rank is not designated, immediately

7.   N. F. Blake, *Caxton and his World*, p. 40.

after the battle at Hexham.[8] Warkworth's Chronicle on the other hand says "King Harry was taken beside a house of religion, in Lancashire, by means of a black monk of Abingdon".[9] Whoever it was who betrayed Henry, the unfortunate monarch was sent on a humiliating progress to London, with his feet tied in his stirrups, and was put in the Tower, where he spent the next five years and appears to have been happy to be freed of the burdens that kingship had put upon him, as the following verses by him, which display more piety than poetry, show.

> Kingdoms are but cares;
>   State is devoid of stay;
> Riches are ready snares,
>   And hasten to decay.
>
> Pleasure's a privy prick
>   Which vice doth still provoke;
> Pomp, unprompt; and fame a flame;
>   Power a smouldering smoke.
>
> Who meaneth to remove the rock
>   Out of the slimy mud,
> Shall mire himself, and hardly 'scape
>   The swelling of the flood.

---

8.   J. C. Giles, *The Chronicles of the White Rose of York* (London: 1843), p. 14.

9.   Giles 1843, p. 108.

CHAPTER 8

The Diplomatist

When we left Caxton in Bruges in May 1466 he was occupied doing what he could to ameliorate the vexatious conditions in which the English colony there found themselves. These were due not only to Philip the Good's unrelenting attitude on the importation of English cloth, but equally to the earl of Warwick's conciliatory policy towards Louis XI, which, though it was aimed at neutralising the danger of a renewed attempt from the Lancastrians under Louis' protection to recover the English throne, served in no way to improve Anglo-Flemish trade relations. Even before this many English merchants had abandoned Bruges as their principal trading base and had migrated to Utrecht. Here, under a treaty dated 20 November 1464, in which Caxton as Governor of the Merchant Adventurers must have had a hand, they were invited to promote regular cloth fairs, the first of which was held in January 1465.

We know that Caxton was in Utrecht in 1464 and 1465, as records preserved there show that passports were issued to him and his servants in those years. For most of the first years of his governorship, Caxton was obliged to act less and less as a merchant on his own behalf and more as a roving trade commissioner. It was a role for which he was evidently fitted, and he was shortly to play it with great effect as one of the agents who finally succeeded in ending the impasse in Bruges. Edward IV had already shown his recognition of Caxton's skill as a diplomatist when he appointed him and Sir William Whitehill to negotiate a new treaty with Philip the Good earlier on.

Edward was also determined to cut his cousin Warwick down to size. Edward, now twenty-two, enjoyed much popularity, not only as a successful soldier, which could always be relied on to endear an

English king to his people, but perhaps as much for his easy-going ways and his love of good-living, women and pageantry. Beneath this he had a streak of utter ruthlessness which enabled him to get his own way when he so desired. Warwick, in thinking he could rule the roost, misunderstood completely the kind of man that Edward had grown into. One great miscalculation he made was to try and choose a wife for Edward. Part of his plan for making peace with Louis was to marry Edward to a French princess, Bona of Savoie, Louis' sister-in-law. To his immense chagrin, and political discomfiture, when the negotiations were well advanced Edward announced that he had already secretly married, on 1 May 1464.

His bride was some four years older than himself, and a widow with two young sons. What made Edward's choice more surprising was that her family and her late husband had been staunch Lancastrians. Her father was Lord Rivers, and her brother Anthony Woodville, the pair who only four years before, in January 1460, had been kidnapped at Sandwich and taken as prisoners to Calais, where they were admonished in no uncertain terms by Salisbury and Warwick – and by Edward himself. Otherwise they were not ill-treated and were soon released to rejoin Henry VI and fight alongside him at Towton. The Yorkists had given no quarter that day, but the two Woodvilles had made their getaway when Margaret and Henry fled the field and the battle was plainly lost.

Baron Rivers had served Henry faithfully for forty years, but now all hope of the house of Lancaster surviving was gone. And like many other hitherto loyal lords he had had enough of the bloody and fruitless contests between the descendants of Edward III. He was no mere turncoat in deciding to submit himself to the king's mercy in the hope of safeguarding the future of his wife and their large family. Edward IV, though merciless in the heat of battle, could be forgiving in victory. He received Lord Rivers graciously, no doubt recognising the worth of a man of such proved, if so far misguided, loyalty.

How Edward came to know Elizabeth Woodville and got round to asking her to marry him can only be guessed at. She could have known him from the day of his birth, as her father was on Richard of York's staff in the Normandy campaign before the final rift between York and Henry VI. The children of the two duchesses,

Cecily of York and Rivers' wife Jacquetta, could well have been playmates in the castle of Rouen, where Edward was born. No authentic likeness of Elizabeth exists, but she cannot have been without her attractions, and it would be pleasant to think that Edward, who already had a liking for the fair sex and would later be a poor model of marital fidelity, fell truly in love with her when years later they met again.[1]

There could be an additional reason for Edward marrying beneath him, as some of his nobles thought he had done, when he could have had the pick not only of much better born English ladies but also of a number of foreign princesses. It would perhaps be an exaggeration to suggest that taking Elizabeth Woodville as his wife was the subtle start of a deliberate move on his part to escape from the constraints that had been placed on him by Warwick and the other magnates who had placed him on the throne. But before long he began to advance Elizabeth's family and their friends to positions of influence. Her father was made Treasurer of England, the post he had earlier held under Henry VI, and in 1466 he was elevated to an earldom. Her brother Anthony had aready become a baron, *jure uxoris*, by marrying Elizabeth Baroness Scales, who had inherited the title, and estates to go with it, of her father who was murdered by Thames watermen in 1460. In 1466 Anthony, like his father earlier on, was made a Knight of the Garter, and donned the blue mantle of that chivalrous order, which in modern times is of velvet, but in those days was of wool, indicating how important the wool trade was to England. In St George's Chapel, Windsor, the metal plate placed over the stall where Anthony Woodville sat is still there to be seen, emblazoned with his coat of arms.

Though it is only later, sometime after 1471, that Sir John Fortescue wrote in his treatise *The Governance of England* of the peril that can come to a king from "over-mighty subjects" this now well-worn expression was meant mainly to describe, and most aptly, Richard Neville earl of Warwick. Edward had already recognised this peril. Not only did he set out to thwart the Kingmaker's plans by every underhand means he could, but by arranging the marriage

---

1. In Queens' College, Cambridge, there is a portrait which is an early Tudor copy of a lost original. A portrait in the British Museum is so different in most details that it could be of a different woman altogether.

of six of Elizabeth's sisters to wealthy peers, he gathered round himself a circle of supporters who provided an effective counter-balance to the following that Warwick could command. Edward was turning out to be as astute a politician as was Warwick, both domestically and in international affairs. He was convinced that an improvement in relations with the Burgundians in Flanders, rather than with France, would be of greater benefit to this country.

France had few commodities other than wine to offer in trade, whereas Flanders was the market where just about everything could be bought and sold. Moreover, in Edward's view an alliance with Burgundy would be a far better way of dealing with the threat from France than either outright war or Warwick's policy of appeasing Louis. For a year or more Philip the Good, now almost senile, had left the government of his realms to his son Charles. Charles was a very different kettle of fish from his father, and though later he was given the more flattering title of Charles the Bold, he was known at first as Charles the Rash. He was itching to retake the Somme towns which his father had acquired under the treaty of Arras but had later sold back in what Charles thought was a poor bargain. It was only a matter of a little time before Charles would become ruler, and Edward saw in him a way of re-opening the negotiations in which Caxton had been concerned earlier, but which had come to nothing because of Philip the Good's obstinacy and Warwick's interfering.

In the autumn of 1465 Charles' wife (his second) died, and again Edward saw that marriage could be a very useful political tool. He not only offered the hand of his sister Margaret to Charles; he also suggested that his brother, George duke of Clarence, should marry Charles' daughter Mary – who if Charles died without a son would inherit the Burgundian dukedom. Charles was not an attractive man either in manner or mien. But dutifully Margaret agreed to be the bait on Edward's line, though it took some time and careful angling before the fish was finally landed. Oddly enough the mis-sion that went to discuss a marriage treaty with Charles was headed by Warwick, and it is not surprising that the initial approach failed. Though he had not succeeded in getting Edward to marry a French princess, Warwick still hoped for a pact with France and in 1467 he put before Edward the names of four other possible suitors for

Margaret, all of them protegés of Louis. Edward took the opportunity that this presented of again snubbing Warwick by turning
down his proposals out of hand. Angered and humiliated, Warwick
set about designing the downfall of Edward.

On 15 June 1467 Philip the Good died, and the new duke expressed his willingness after all to marry Margaret – on certain conditions. One was that a large force of English archers was to be put at
his disposal for the campaign he now planned to open against Louis
XI. To this Edward readily agreed, for if Louis was kept busy
fighting off Charles he would be less able to assist Margaret of
Anjou in any attempt to rescue Henry VI from the Tower and
restore him to the throne. Henry's queen had been a refugee at
Louis' court since fleeing there after the battle of Hexham, and
Louis had already financed various minor insurrections on her
behalf.

One of these, led by Jasper Tudor, earl of Pembroke and Henry's
half-brother, occurred in June 1468, and in order to deal with it
Edward was obliged to stay in England and was unable to accompany his sister when she set off on 18 June for her marriage to
Charles. Instead Edward nominated Anthony Woodville his
brother-in-law to give the bride away.

The marriage was solemnised with great splendour in the
Stadhuis at Damme at the unearthly hour of five in the morning of
2 July, and was followed by ten days of festivities. What part William Caxton had in these is not recorded. As governor of the
English community in Flanders he would be a participant, but not
to the extent that Blades makes out, and it is most unlikely that it
was at this time that he attracted the attention of the new duchess.[2]
He would be found a place at one of the tables in the great banquet-
ing hall, but as a commoner and a mere merchant he would remain
respectfully on the fringe of the throng of nobles who had accompanied Margaret from England. So neither at this time would he
make the acquaintance of Anthony Woodville, though later both
Margaret and Anthony were to become his patrons and friends.

It was only when the nuptials were over that Caxton was to
resume his place of authority. Edward hoped for much out of the
marriage he had arranged for his favourite sister. On 9 September

---

2. Blades 1877 p. 25.

1468 the Court of Adventurers, at the desire of "the kynge and his Counsell", appointed three of their members to renew negotiations with the duke of Burgundy and endeavour to put an end to the differences that had for so many years bedevilled trade between the two countries.

The three were William Redeknape, John Pickering and William Caxton. On 28 September the court advanced Redeknape and Pickering £40 "towarde thoire costs & charges", but there is no mention of any such disbursement to Caxton, who being already on the spot in Bruges would not require any expenses.[3] The success of this mission has often been described as a diplomatic triumph for Caxton, but in reality it was a foregone conclusion. The duke of Burgundy personally gained many benefits by marrying Margaret, including a large dowry, but implicit in the marriage contract was an undertaking that he would recognise the rights of the English merchants in Flanders. All that Caxton and the two other envoys had to do was to settle the details. The outcome was a broad-based treaty, signed in October, that was to run for thirty years, or so it was sanguinely agreed.

It seemed that fortune had at last favoured Edward. His shrewd move had checked Warwick at home and had, again it seemed, ended the threat from Louis XI and Margaret of Anjou. But he had still to have a final showdown with over-mighty Warwick, who from Calais, of which he still held the captaincy, was in traitorous communication with Louis. He was also able to lure Edward's weak-willed brother George duke of Clarence to join him in Calais, and on 11 July 1469 married him to his elder daughter Isobel. The idea was that having overthrown Edward he would be kingmaker again and could put the pliable Clarence on the throne, thereby becoming the effective ruler of England.

Financed by Louis, Warwick instigated a series of risings in the Midlands. The most serious of these culminated in the battle of Edgcote on 26 July, at which Edward was captured. Fighting alongside Edward was his father-in-law Earl Rivers, and Rivers' second son John. To these representatives of the hated Woodville faction which had supplanted him in Edward's regard, Warwick showed no mercy and had them beheaded. Thus Anthony Wood-

---

3. Blades 1877 p. 149 prints these two minutes in full.

ville, Caxton's friend and patron, became the second Earl Rivers. Warwick realised he could not take such extreme measures with Edward. Edward was popular with the people at large and had too many supporters in London for Warwick to assume there the role for which he had cast himself. After two months Edward was released. Knowing that he could not take action against Warwick without also arraigning his brother Clarence, Edward overlooked the indignity he had suffered, and by December 1469 the conniving pair were back at Westminster as though nothing had happened.

With mole-like industry however Warwick was still engaged in undermining Edward's position. Unexpectedly in March 1470 there was another rebellious eruption in Lincolnshire and Edward hurried north. Warwick and Clarence promised to follow hard behind him with reinforcements. Before they could do so Edward had defeated the rebels in a fierce skirmish at Empingham. The local leader, Sir Robert Welles, was summarily tried and executed – but he first revealed that Warwick and Clarence were behind the rising and that the reinforcements they had promised were meant for the rebels, not for Edward. Before Edward could call them to account the two conspirators fled the country, but the discredited Warwick was refused entry to Calais and they were obliged to make for Honfleur instead.

Louis XI received them with a cynical show of welcome, though they were greeted less amiably by the Lancastrian émigrés at the French court. Margaret of Anjou openly rejoiced over Warwick's sorry situation. Eventually however she was persuaded by Louis that with a commander like Warwick beside her, and with French ships and funds, she would at last have a real opportunity of regaining the English throne for her husband. Ready to grasp at any means of getting even with Edward, Warwick offered with nicely simulated contrition to make amends for his former treatment of her. He undertook to champion her cause unreservedly, and as a token of his allegiance to the house of Lancaster his second daughter and co-heiress Anne was married to Margaret's son, the young Prince of Wales. As he saw it, even if he threw Clarence aside, here was yet another chance that a daughter of his might become the English queen and that he would be able to pull strings from behind her skirts.

On 13 September 1470 Warwick's French ships landed in Devonshire. A feint attack had led Edward to expect Warwick's invasion to be made somewhere along the east coast, and he hurried to repel it. When he realised that he had been fooled he turned about, only to find that the larger part of his army under John Neville marquess of Montagu, who was Warwick's brother but had pretended to be loyal to Edward, had stolen away and deserted him. There was nothing he could do except take ship across the North Sea for Holland if he were to avoid capture by Warwick again. With Edward went a few faithful friends, his other brother, Richard duke of Gloucester, and his brother-in-law Anthony Woodville, now Earl Rivers. From Holland he made his way to Bruges, but at first Charles the Bold showed no inclination to help his wife's brother, who might become a liability. For three months he refused Edward an audience. It was only when his intelligence agents advised him that Louis XI's real objective in assisting Warwick and Margaret of Anjou was to make possible a joint Anglo-French invasion of the Burgundian domains in Flanders that Charles agreed to supply Edward with ships, money and men.

Landing in Yorkshire on 14 March 1471 with 1200 Burgundian merceneries Edward was immediately joined by local partisans who had remained loyal to the Yorkist cause. Montagu, who had left him in the lurch the previous September, was holed up with a small army in Pontefract Castle and made no move to bar his way. Marching south and gaining recruits as he went, Edward slyly by-passed Coventry where Warwick had six or seven thousand men at readiness, and made for London, where on 11 April he was welcomed by the mayor and aldermen. They and the City merchants remembered with gratitude how Edward had striven for improved trade relations with their Flemish counterparts. In London, too, his queen proudly showed him his son and heir who had been born in sanctuary at Westminster, where she had been left unmolested while Edward was a refugee in Bruges. In a brief ceremony in the Abbey Edward symbolically placed the crown on his own head again, and Henry VI was handed over to him. He looked at the pathetic Henry with pity, but this did not prevent him from taking Henry, a listless and prematurely old man of fifty, with him as a trophy when on 13 April, Easter Saturday, he marched out of

London to do battle with Warwick, who had followed him from Coventry and was now encamped near Barnet. Early on Easter Day Edward attacked under cover of thick fog, and for a time it was uncertain how the battle was going, but after about four hours of confusion as isolated groups of the two armies encountered one another and fought separate little battles, victory went to Edward. The next day Warwick's corpse was found and carried to London, where it was put on show to prove to all that Edward was truly king once more. Henry VI was put back in the Tower.

Margaret of Anjou was still to be reckoned with. As distrustful of Warwick as ever, she had been in no hurry to answer his call to come and join her husband after Edward had fled to Holland. When finally she did arrive it was on the day that Warwick met his death. Accompanied by the seventeen years old Prince of Wales and a force of French troops she landed at Weymouth, and linking up with Edmund duke of Somerset she started off on 15 April to join Jasper Tudor, who was gathering an army for her in Wales. To do this she had to cross the river Severn at Tewkesbury.

It was here that Edward, having anticipated her intention, intercepted her on 4 May. The battle of Tewkesbury was a massacre; 2000 men perished in the fighting. So did many of the Lancastrian nobles, and the day after the battle eighteen more were executed, including Somerset, who was dragged out of sanctuary in Tewkesbury Abbey on the grounds that as a traitor (to Edward that is) he had no right to sanctuary. The Prince of Wales was killed in the midst of the fray, so that there remained now only one person with any possible pretensions to the Lancastrian throne. This was young Henry Tudor, who was in Wales with his uncle Jasper. Guided by Jasper the future Henry VII escaped to Brittany, where he stayed fourteen years before returning to put a decisive end to the Wars of the Roses at Bosworth, and to unite the houses of York and Lancaster by marrying Edward IV's daughter Elizabeth.

Margaret of Anjou was captured three days after the battle, and on 21 May was paraded by Edward in a triumphal procession through London. That same day Henry VI died in the Tower, a suspiciously convenient coincidence for Edward, and another of the black deeds attributed to Richard of Gloucester. The unhappy Margaret, broken by the death of her darling son and her husband, was kept in a series of reasonably comfortable prisons until 1475, when Louis XI ransomed her and she retired to her native Anjou, where she died in 1482 at the age of fifty-three.

CHAPTER 9

The Courtier

During the two years in which England was being torn apart by the self-seeking Warwick's campaign against Edward IV, William Caxton's life in Bruges followed a much more steady tenor. Under the terms of the favourable new trade treaty which had resulted from the marriage of Charles the Bold and Edward's sister, and which Caxton was partly instrumental in concluding, Bruges became once more the principal English staple in north-west Europe, far more important than Calais. Since the accession of Louis XI trade between England and France had virtually ceased and Calais had become more a military enclave than a commercial depot. Accordingly one of Caxton's first tasks was to bring back the English merchants who earlier had transferred their businesses to Utrecht in protest at the restrictions imposed on them at Bruges.

Caxton himself had remained at Bruges, though as he was subject to the same restrictions he cannot have done much business as a mercer, and any trading he did would have to be in other goods than cloth. In any case, having been appointed Governor of the English Nation of Merchant Adventurers in the Low Countries he would have little time to spare from the duties of that office to attend to business on his own account. The post would require him to pay frequent visits to the various towns of the Low Countries in which English merchants were operating, and he was probably absent from Bruges as often as he was present.

Apart from this he had to contend with problems arising from the competition that his fellow countrymen had to meet from the Hanseatic League, a powerful federation of German merchants who for two centuries had had a firm grip on trade in Flanders. The "Company of German Merchants in Bruges", whose statutes were drawn up in 1347, enjoyed far greater privileges than the English community. The resentment of the English merchants was all the stronger because the Hanseatics were also the most numerous group of alien merchants in England, with posts at York, Hull, Ipswich, Norwich, Yarmouth, Bristol and London. In Caxton's time the hanse in London, called the Steelyard (from the massive beam-balance used for weighing goods there), had jurisdiction over the others, a right granted in 1422. The London hanse was the first to be founded in England and had been established by merchants from Cologne.

When the rivalry between the English and the German merchants came to a head it erupted into actual warfare in the form of attacks on each other's ships and blockades of ports, a situation that lasted from 1469 to 1474. It was Edward IV's zeal for promoting concord with Burgundy that started the conflict. Partly to please the London merchants, who had been generous contributors to the Yorkist cause and were jealous of the privileges accorded to the Germans, but more in order to please the Flemings, he had refused to renew the charter of the London hanse except on a year to year basis. In 1468, to give a fillip to the negotiations that Caxton was conducting for the new Anglo–Flemish agreement, he ordered the Steelyard to be closed down. It was not a politic gesture and it provoked the naval actions just mentioned, as well as a total prohibition on the sale of English cloth in all Hanseatic towns.

Cologne was the only town that defied the Hanseatic Council and did not break off relations with England – a circumstance that was to be of benefit to Caxton when he seriously took up printing. It also resulted in Cologne being expelled from the League in 1470, but the immediate upshot was that Edward reversed his attitude towards the London hanse, which consisted mainly of merchants from Cologne, and allowed the Steelyard to be reopened. This did not however make the task of Caxton any easier in Bruges, as he said in a brisk letter to the Court of Common Council in London. Caxton in the negotiations that led to the treaty of October 1468 was supposed to seek not only the lifting of the ban on English cloth, but also parity of conditions with the Hanseatic merchants in Flanders. This is consistent with the minute of the Court of Adventurers of 28 September 1468 which refers to the "enlargyng of woollen clothe in the Duke of Burgundy's landes", an expression which is much more than a simple instruction to secure a better import quota for English material.

Though Charles the Bold regarded the squabbles of the traders in his city with indifference, and would leave most of the talking to his ministers, he would be bound at times to take part in the discussions, and Caxton would be known to him as the leader of the English delegates. At the conclusion of the conference there would be a formal celebration of some sort, whatever the terms that had been agreed; foreign affairs were conducted with the same urbanity then as they are today. It was on such an occasion that most probably he was presented to Charles' wife Margaret.

In many ways Caxton was something of a snob. There are distinct hints of this in his prologues, and his use of the "humility formula" is not entirely feigned or conventional. No one could have been more pleased or flattered by the condescension towards him of the highest lady of the Burgundian court. His feelings however were tinged with a measure of self-interest as well as an innocent wish to be received at court. Though he was delighted to move up into such circles, he was not such a hypocrite as not to tell himself that Margaret was an excellent business connexion which he could develop to his own advantage.

Margaret too gained something from her acquaintance with Caxton. She knew that her marriage was an empty shell, and that she had been a pawn in a power game. From the start Charles left her very much to herself, though he was but thirty-three and she was twenty-two. Hearne's Fragment records that on the wedding night the castle at Mâle to which they had repaired was set on fire "by treason" when they were both in bed and they had a narrow escape.[1] Other reports say that Charles went to bed alone and there have been suggestions that he was impotent. Though he had been married twice before, the first time was when he was a boy of six. It was a political marriage of convenience, and his infant bride died before it could be consummated. He married again when he was twenty-two, and when Margaret became his third wife he had a daughter of thirteen.

---

1. J. C. Giles, *The Chronicles of the White Rose of York* (London: 1843), p. 20.

Perhaps he was not so much impotent as inhibited by his recollection of the excesses of his father Philip the Good, who in spite of his name had thirty known mistresses and a tally of seventeen bastards. Charles was his only legitimate son. Like many martial figures in history Charles was more interested in war than in sex. Whatever the reason for his neglect of Margaret any doubts regarding his virility cannot have been known to Edward IV, as the marriage contract that had been drawn up made provision for Margaret's children, which never came.

After the excitement of the marriage festivities died down and the English nobles returned home Margaret was on her own except for the company of the ladies in waiting who remained with her, and of her mother-in-law Isabella of Portugal, with whom she got on well, and her step-daughter Mary of Burgundy, for whom, being herself childless, she showed a genuine affection. The bleakness of her married life was made more tolerable by the fact that she was a woman of deep piety. An illumination in a manuscript in the Bodleian Library, Oxford, shows her at prayer,[2] and her preoccupation with religion is indicated by similar illuminations in other manuscripts.

The everyday language of the Burgundian court would have no difficulties for her as people of her class were fluent in French. All the same there were times when she and her English companions would lapse into their mother tongue, and on the occasions when she met Caxton it would be a pleasant change to converse with him in English, though Caxton for all his protestations of his "unperfightness" in French had a good command of the language.[3] All the translations he later printed were from French originals, with three exceptions – *The Historye of Reynart the Foxe* (from Dutch), *The Lyf of Saynt Wenefryde* and *The Craft for to Dye* (from Latin), though it should be added that there are doubts as to his authorship of the last named. Caxton's contacts with Margaret's husband would be few and concerned only with matters that called for the duke's personal attention or presence.

One of these would be on 4 February 1470 when Charles was invested with the order of the Garter in an imposing ceremony at

2.   MS Douce 365, fol. 115.
3.   Prologue to the *Recuyell*.

Ghent. Edward IV was at that time tied down in England by the troubles that Warwick was stirring up, and the investiture was performed on his behalf by Sir Thomas Vaughan and the Garter King at Arms. A Latin oration made at the service by Dr John Russell, "Archdiacre de Berksuir" and later Bishop of Lincoln, was one of the first publications produced by Caxton when he took up printing.

Caxton's meetings with Margaret on the other hand were much more frequent, and by all accounts she took delight in the company of the homely and unpresuming merchant who treated her with such grave, and sometimes amusing, deference. Though he was undistinguished socially, as doyen of the English colony in Bruges Caxton would be invited to court functions and receptions. Beyond this there seems to have grown up an indulgent and innocent relationship between the high-born lady and the mature and older man, which sprang from her sense of isolation and helped to sustain her in the early years of her exile. She would be impressed by his knowledge of the ways of the world too, and his long experience as a businessman would be useful to her in the management of her affairs.

The idea however that somewhere around this time Caxton entered the duchess's full-time service as her financial advisor or in any other capacity, as many biographers before and after Blades have led us to believe, is without foundation. When he describes himself as a "servant unto her said grace" in his prologue to the *Recuyell* it is nothing more than a touch of smarm. There are numerous instances where Caxton calls himself the "humble servant" of his patrons. One is in his dedication of *The Game and Playe of the Chesse* to George duke of Clarence, whom he did not even know and in whose service he could not have been. And though he received certain fees from Margaret these were more than likely in recognition of occasional kindnesses he was able to render her, such as supervising the clearance of goods through the customs, over which he had control. They may not even have gone into his own pocket, but could have been the usual charges for performing such functions. The word "fee" has a diversity of meanings. The payments to Caxton could have been in kind rather than cash and simply a token of esteem from Margaret, in the same way as later, when Caxton was putting together his version of *The Golden Legend*, William earl of Arundel gave him a "yerely fee" of a buck in summer and a doe in winter as a mark of encouragement.[4] Margaret was never his employer in the strict sense of the word, but as far as class barriers allowed she became his fond friend.

In one special respect Caxton could have been of great service to Margaret. She was a woman of exceptional intelligence, which even her boorish husband recognised, and to while away the time she became an avid reader. In the ducal palace at Bruges there was the large library built up by Philip the Good,[5] but her own taste was for books of devotions and moral works rather than the tales of chivalry which were mainly the vogue. The manuscript with a likeness of her at prayer which we have mentioned is *Traités de morale et religion*, written by David Aubert, Philip's amanuensis, who was still around the court. At Margaret's request he wrote several other tracts, and her almoner Nicholas Finet translated for her *Benois seront les miséricordieux*.

Her merchant friend Caxton was well placed to indulge her appetite for reading, as the interchange of manuscripts had become a sizable element in overseas trade. Through him she would be able to obtain manuscripts in her native tongue from London, where the extent of this trade can be gauged from the growing importance of the Stationers' Company. The part that the merchants played is acknowledged by John Bagford, who in the early eighteenth century was the first writer to attempt to compile a definitive biography of Caxton, though it was never published. "Kings, Queens and noblemen", he wrote, "had their particular merchants who, when they were ready for their voyage into foreign parts, sent their servants to know what they wanted, and, among the rest of their choice, many times books were demanded."[6]

That Caxton shared Margaret's zest for reading is unlikely. He was an educated man, but his attitude towards books was not that of a dedicated scholar, at least not at this stage of his life, if ever. As a hard-working man of business he had other calls on his time, and the suggestion that he had literary pretensions from an early age

---

4. Blades 1877 p. 81; Crotch 1928 p. 70.
5. v.s. p. 79.
6. Bagford's remnants are now in the British Museum (MS Harley 5919).

and that the *Recuyell* was not his first essay in translation, as one biographer has tried to make out, is merely fanciful.[7] Why Caxton eventually took on this particular task has been explained in a variety of ways.

His own explanation in the prologue to Book I is that it was to prevent him falling into habits of sloth and idleness. Idleness he regarded as "the mother and nourisher of vices", and to fight off any inclination towards it he felt obliged to direct himself "unto vertuous occupation and business". This does not ring true, and sounds like another example of the conventional phraseology used by authors of those days, and has a distinct echo of the words used by Raoul Lefèvre, who translated the version that Caxton used from Latin in 1464 for Philip the Good. Caxton was never given to idling and was still hard at work when he drew his last breath, as is shown by Wynken de Worde's colophon to the *Vitae Patrum* (printed 1495) which he says was "translated out of Frenche into Englisshe by William Caxton of Westmynstre late dead and fynysshed at the laste day of hys lyff".

One good reason why Caxton could not have been in Margaret's full-time employ was that he was still Governor of the Merchant Adventurers, and for the same reason he would have had little time to spare for literary pursuits unless he thought that they might later prove profitable. A widely held notion regarding Caxton is that he was imbued with a love of the ideals of chivalry and that this is exemplified by the large number of tales of knightly valour that are among the books he later chose for printing. The *Recuyell* is certainly such a book, but he was no romantic and his choice of it could have been quite fortuitous. There could have been just a touch of vanity in his setting out to translate it, in the hope of impressing his dear duchess, but his real reason was probably a much more hard-headed one. One possible reason for his choosing it was that Lefèvre's version was immediately to hand in the ducal library. Margaret could well have loaned it to him, or at least a scrivener's copy of it, as he records that he had it with him in Ghent in 1471 and in Cologne that same year when he finished his translation on 19 September.

---

7.   H. R. Plomer, *William Caxton 1424–1491* (Parsons, London: 1925), p. 175.

Whatever his reason for venturing into the literary field he tells us in the prologue that he started his translation on 1 March 1469, and after completing five or six quires he laid it aside, being dissatisfied, he would have us believe, with his efforts and disheartened by his poor command of English. For him to have got so far with it is indicative of Caxton's energetic application to everything he tackled; each quire would consist of eight or ten leaves and he had therefore penned between forty to sixty leaves of manuscript. Something more than Caxton's modesty is required to explain why he abandoned his project, for everything else he undertook he held to with a characteristic tenacity.

The duties of his office as governor were still onerous, and conscientious man that he was he would not have neglected them even if he could have. They involved much travel, and within a little more than two months of his starting on his translation he was off on one of his trips. This is seen from the record of a civil action dated 12 May 1469 in which Caxton as "governour des marchans d'angleterre" should have acted as arbitrator between an Englishman and a Genoese merchant, but because "the said William Caxton was unavoidably absent from the said city of Bruges" judgment was given by the full court of merchants.[8]

Like so many other occasions in Caxton's life the date of his relinquishing the governorship can only be guessed at. He was presumably present in that capacity when Margaret's husband was made a Knight of the Garter on 4 February 1470, and the town records of Middelburg for the same year refer to him as "Willem Caxstoen, meester van der Ingelsche nacie".[9] In the autumn of 1470 the contentions between Warwick and Edward IV culminated in Edward's flight to Bruges. Edward and his followers arrived with little more than the clothes they stood up in, and during the three months that Charles kept them waiting about they were obliged to turn to the English community in Bruges for maintenance and financial assistance.

As governor Caxton would be mainly responsible for organising this relief, and he would, probably for the first time, come to the personal notice of the king. Though Edward was never the great

---

8. Blades 1877 pp. 157–8 gives a translation of the full judgment.
9. Crotch 1928 p. cxxxviii.

patron of Caxton that has been made out and showed only slight interest in his printing venture, he came to trust Caxton and engaged him on several diplomatic and commercial missions in the course of the next few years. Various payments to Caxton recorded in the Issue Rolls of the Exchequer probably relate to these. A payment of £20 dated 15 June 1480 (19 Edw. 4), is "for certain causes and matters performed by him for the said Lord the King" and Blades asks: "Might not this have been for assistance to Edward IV and his retinue when fugitives at Bruges?"[10] If so the king's expression of his gratitude seems to have been somewhat belated, and in asking his question Blades is giving loose rein to his imagination. The cryptic expression "certain causes and matters" used in the entry in the Exchequer Roll just quoted indicates the confidential nature of the missions that Caxton undertook, and explains why no details of them are to be found.

Caxton was acting as Edward's agent as late as 1475, and something of what he was doing is known from other sources. Charles the Bold was still hankering for a war with France, but after the death of Warwick at Barnet Edward had set his heart on restoring prosperity and harmony in England and was reluctant to embroil his country in any such mad scheme. He had treaty obligations to Charles however. Besides, the temper of the people was all for having a crack at their old enemy and parliament voted money for an expeditionary force to be sent to Calais. Charles was to send a fleet of Dutch yawls to transport the English troops, and one of the commissaries appointed to collect the boats was William Caxton, who in April 1475 visited Delft, Rotterdam, Flushing and other Dutch towns for this purpose. He makes what might be a reference to this expedition when he speaks of Edward "conqueryng his rightfull inheritance".[11] Edward crossed to Calais on 4 July, but in the event Charles' rash venture fizzled out and Edward made a separate and very satisfactory truce with Louis XI, who bought him off with a down payment of 75,000 crowns and a "pension" of 50,000 crowns annually.

Caxton's time between 1470 and 1475 was not entirely taken up by the commissions that Edward gave him or his routine duties as

---

10.   Blades 1877 pp. 80 and 158.
11.   Epilogue to *The Game and Playe of the Chesse.*

governor and in trying to settle the dispute with the Hanseatic League. In March 1471 Edward left Bruges to recover his kingdom from Warwick, and Caxton was able to turn his attention again to his efforts at translating Lefèvre's manuscript. He says in his prologue that though he had fallen "in despair of this work and purposed no more to have continued therein . . . on a time it fortuned that my Lady Margaret sent for me to speak of divers matters, among the which I let her highness have knowledge of the aforesaid beginning of this work; which anon commanded me to show the said five or six quires to her said grace. And when she had seen them, anon she found default in mine English, which she commanded me to amend, and moreover commanded me straightly to continue and make an end of the residue not then translated. Whose dreadful commandment I durst in no wise disobey."

Caxton's English, though he more than once decries it, was probably as good as that of the duchess, but deferring to her was part of a plan that Caxton had conceived and at which we have already hinted. As a man of wide-ranging business interests he would keep himself acquainted with what was taking place in the world around him, and in his early days in Bruges he would have heard of a novel way of reproducing copies of manuscripts in large numbers which had been developed in Mainz in Germany round about the year 1450. He says so in his addition to the *Polychronicon*: "About this time the craft of printing was first found in Mogunce[12] in Almayne."

At first he may not have recognised the significance of this information. Later as he observed the appreciable trade in manuscripts that was going on and in which he took part as a side-line, the idea gradually entered his mind that the trade could be put on a really profitable footing if printed copies of manuscripts, almost identical with the laboriously handwritten originals but cheaper by far to produce, were available to him. And if he were to produce these copies himself, rather than buy them from the people who had already set up as printers, his profit margin would be all the greater. When he saw the first printed books that began to arrive in Bruges and was able to examine them, he noticed that almost without exception they were classical Latin texts or occasionally a Greek

---

12.   From the Roman name for Mainz – *Moguntiacum*.

one. He might also have seen a copy of Gutenberg's great Bible for which Johannes Fust had set about promoting sales. But there were few books if any in Gutenberg's own language, and none at all in French, as the art of printing did not reach Paris until 1470.

In its first years printing was almost exclusively the servant of the New Learning and the first printers ignored the vernacular languages of Europe. In this Caxton was not slow to see an opportunity on which he could capitalise, for in England there was an assured market waiting if he could produce in English the sort of books that the literate classes wanted. As he toyed with the idea its attractions grew, though he was too busy with other matters to put it into practice immediately, as we have said above.

But in March 1471 his term of office as Governor of the Merchant Adventurers was almost over, though he would still have occasional duties laid on him by Edward almost up to the time when he finally left Bruges and returned to England. So when in the course of discussing other matters with Margaret he craftily "let her highness have knowledge" of the project he had embarked on two years before and she "straightly commanded him to continue and make an end of the residue not then translated", he did so with alcrity and within six months had completed his translation. He says that he "durst in no wise disobey" his lady's commandment, but the real reason for this burst of energy was that he knew the circumstances were right for him to proceed with his plans for printing books in English and for eventually setting up a press in Westminster – not as something to occupy his declining years (he was only about fifty), but as a business which had a good chance of paying off handsomely. That this is the reason why he tried his hand at translation is the only plausible one.

He was no dilettante and would not have turned to writing simply as a pastime. Nor is he entirely to be believed when he says that he learned to print because he had promised copies of the *Recuyell* "to divers gentlemen and my friends".[13] For that purpose he could have employed a professional scribe to make sufficient copies. The truth is that right from the start his aim was to produce books in quantity for sale and he intended that the *Recuyell* should be the first of many books that he intended to print. Why he did not content

13. Epilogue to Book III.

himself with printing an existing classical text as most of the early printers did, or one of the many French manuscripts that were available to him in Bruges, is because he had his eyes on the potential market that he thought existed for books in English, and which no one yet had thought of exploiting. As for why he decided to make the translation himself instead of giving the job to a professional translator, he probably considered that there was no one in Bruges who was any more able to turn a French text into English than he was himself, even though he had no practical experience so far as a translator or as a writer for publication. We have already more or less concluded that the misgivings that Caxton expressed regarding his literary ability contained a fair measure of false modesty. Apart however from the difficulty of finding anyone else who could produce a satisfactory translation for him, another reason was that he was keeping his cards close to his chest, and he was careful not to divulge his cherished dream of being England's first printer to anyone, for fear of being forestalled.

His assiduous cultivation of Margaret's friendship was also part of his plan, and when he was sure of her interest and patronage he went straight into action to bring it to fruition. In his heart he probably cared little about the faults that she found in his English or for the suggestions she made to improve it, if indeed she made any. What he wanted was permission to dedicate his book to her. What better testimonial could it have? At Margaret's court Englishmen of quality came and went constantly, many of whom were the sort of readers for whom he hoped to cater and who would take copies of his book back to England and possibly create a demand for it there. Though a book that had been written "at the command" of the English-born duchess would attract a number of customers among the English merchants in Bruges, Caxton also had high hopes of the English home market, in which his business connexions would enable him to dispose of his *Recuyell,* and of other books he would print, in quantities that would make his printing venture worthwhile.

His intention was to go into the book business in a big way, and he studied his market carefully. The books he later chose for publication at Westminster were what he thought would be best sellers - romances of chivalry and knighthood, popular poetry, and books of devotions, which sold well in those less irreligious days. Occasionally he did odd job printing, things like indulgences, but for these he would be paid outright and he took no publishing risks with them. The first known work he printed in England was an indulgence, a modest job which would enable him to flex his muscles and try out his newly erected press before he ventured on to lengthier publications. Classical Latin and Greek texts he left to others to print, and his press played no part at all in the spreading of Renaissance ideals in England. But he did not neglect entirely the demand for such books and his contacts with the Continent enabled him to obtain these and other publications quickly to order. In fact the importing of books appears to have represented a substantial part of his turnover.[14] In becoming a printer Caxton had not ceased to be a merchant; he had simply adopted another line in merchandise.

---

14.   K. J. M. Kerling, *Caxton and the Trade in Printed Books* (The Book Collector, iv, 1955, pp. 190–9).

Caxton's device or trade-mark, first used in 1487 on
the last page of a Sarum Missal, the printing of
which Caxton sub-contracted to Guillaume
Maynyal in Paris as he himself lacked the
appropriate typefaces. To indicate that he was the
publisher Caxton had this mark engraved and
overprinted it on the last page on the sheets
produced by Maynyal, which happened to be
blank. The interlaced lines between the letters W
and C were once thought to be the figures 74, by
which it was supposed that Caxton was
commemorating the printing of the *Recuyell* in
1474, but this is unlikely as Caxton nowhere else
used arabic figures. They are now considered to be
simply a decorative element.

CHAPTER 10

The Printer

Once Caxton had obtained the promise of Margaret's patronage after showing her the first five or six quires of his translation, he made it his next priority to look into the possibility of printing it – even before he had completed the remainder. He was still busy on official duties which involved travelling, but when after his interview with Margaret he left Bruges to visit Ghent, he took with him his copy of Lefèvre's manuscript and his unfinished translation. His next port of call was Cologne, and here he put the finishing touches to his work on 19 September 1471.

In 1470 Cologne had been expelled from the Hanseatic League for refusing to sever her trade relations with England, and the reason for Caxton's visit was on the face of it to cement and extend these bonds. However Caxton was also able to turn the fact that he was welcome in Cologne to his personal advantage. The sack of Mainz, Gutenberg's birthplace, in 1462 by the armies of two rival archbishops who each wanted the see, had resulted in many of its citizens going into voluntary exile, taking with them the art of printing to other towns and countries. The first town after Mainz to have a printing press was Cologne, fifty or so miles further down the Rhine. That Caxton had ever been in Cologne before is unlikely as Cologne is some two hundred miles distant from Bruges. But an entry dated 17 July 1471 in the town's Register of Aliens shows that he was then given a permit to reside there for three months. The permit was renewed three times, and he remained in Cologne without a break until the end of 1472, a period of eighteen months in all.[1]

Some Caxton scholars, Blades in particular, express strong doubts as to whether it was in Cologne that Caxton learned to

1. J. C. Birch, *William Caxton's Stay at Cologne* (The Library, 4th Series, iv, 1923–4, pp. 50–52).

print, and he himself never actually claims to have done so.[2] But as Cologne after 1464 rapidly became the major centre of printing in western Europe, and in view of his desire to go into business as a printer, it seems only natural that while there he would take the opportunity of picking up all the knowledge he could about the craft. The case for Caxton having learned the art of printing during his stay in Cologne has been argued conclusively by a later scholar.[3]

At the time Caxton was in Cologne several printers were in business there. The first of these to have started up was Ulrich Zell, who brought a press with him from Mainz, and some founts of type based on a distinctive script that had long been in use by scribes in the archdiocese of Mainz. He is thought by some to have taught Caxton the trade, but Blades disputes this and insists that the quality of Caxton's press work and the design of the earlier types he used were much inferior to those of the Cologne school of printing.[4] On these grounds Blades waxes emphatic in his views that Caxton did not learn his printing in Cologne – in spite of the fact that Wynken de Worde in the "prohemium" to his edition of an English translation of Bartholemaeus's *De Proprietatubus Rerum* printed about 1495 wrote:

And also of your charyte call to remembraunce
    The soule of William Caxton, first printer of this boke
    In Laten tongue at Coleyn . . .

As this does not fit with Blades' pet theories he dismisses de Worde's evidence out of hand, with the stern words: 'Now this seems to be merely a careless statement of Wynken de Worde; for if Caxton did really print "Bartholemaeus" in that city, it must have been with his own types and presses, as the workmanship of his early volumes proves that he had no connection with the Cologne printers, whose practices were entirely different'.[5]

---

2. Blades 1877 devotes the whole of Chapter VI to this argument.

3. Henry Thomas, *Wilh. Caxton uyss Engelant. Evidence that the first English Printer learned his craft at Cologne* (Privately printed at Cologne, 1928, in a limited edition of 200 for the Monotype Corporation and presented to a visiting delegation of English master printers).

4. Blades 1877 pp. 44, 62, 63.

5. Blades 1877 p. 65.

Blades is not even ready to admit that an edition of *De Proprietatibus Rerum* was produced at Cologne during Caxton's stay there, and goes to great length to make this point. "The time necessary for the production of so extensive a work would have been considerable," he says. Whereas, he goes on, Caxton's stay "was but short". Almost grudgingly he agrees that "there is more than one old undated edition belonging to the German school of printing", but implies that these were produced later. There is however a copy in the British Museum which has been authenticated as having been printed in Cologne at the time that Caxton was there, and this he could well have seen on the press or even have had a hand in the printing of it.[6] A glaring *non sequitur* in Blades' strictures on Wynken de Worde is his statement that "if Caxton did really print 'Bartholemaeus' in that city, it must have been with his own types and presses." Though the printers of Cologne would not encourage competition for themselves in their own city they did not maintain such a "closed shop" that they would object to the English visitor looking over their shoulder as they worked, nor would regard him as a potential business rival.

On the contrary Cologne had a long-standing trade relationship with England and Caxton and his fellow-merchants had proved a useful channel of distribution for the books they printed. Caxton was a person they would seek to humour. Perhaps he did not disclose to them his plans for setting up on his own as a printer, but if he did let on that he hoped to print books in English this would not seem to them to endanger their own interests. And if he wanted to learn to print at his own "charge and expense" (as he put it in the prologue to the *Recuyell*) they would be only too willing to admit him to their shops and give him lessons. Therefore he would not necessarily have needed type and presses of his own.

Only at the end of 1472 when he left Cologne would he need to acquire some founts of type or matrices from which to cast them, and to take these with him. A printing press and other equipment, such as ink-balls and type-cases, could be made for him locally in Bruges. A suggestion has been made that even as early as this an element of demarcation between different sections of the printing

---

6. *Catalogue of Books Printed in the XVth Century now in the British Museum* (reprinted 1963), I, 234–5.

trade had begun to emerge. Printers were still for the most part printer-publishers, responsible for the physical production and selection of the titles they published and for their distribution and sale, though sometimes they would be commissioned to print an occasional volume for a wealthy patron. But the making of paper, on the other hand, was a separate craft from an early date once it had largely replaced vellum, and not all printers cast their own type. Smaller printers and newcomers to the industry would obtain founts from larger printers.

There is also more than a possibility that already in Cologne there was a specialised type-founding business or even a printers' general supply house, which catered not only for a local demand but exported type and other materials to more distant printing centres. This could have been the source from which Caxton bought the types he took back to Bruges. The brain behind this enterprise is supposed to have been Johannes Veldener, who is known to have been a type-founder at Cologne and to have supplied type to a number of printers there.[7] He was also a printer on his own account, and later became a printer-publisher at Louvain at roughly the time that Caxton was printing in Bruges, where he supplied him with further founts of type.

Just as the production of manuscripts had been a labour of love by monastic scribes, much of the impetus behind early printing came from religious bodies. In spite of what has gone before, Caxton, who to judge from his own writings was a devout man, could have received his first lessons in printing from monkish practitioners of the art. When he stopped off at Ghent on his way to Cologne he lodged at a Benedictine monastery, or so it is said. He cannot have learned anything about printing there, as the art had not yet reached Flanders and would not do so until he himself introduced it from Cologne. Ulrich Zell is reputed to have been a priest, but a secular one rather than a member of a religious order, and no evidence of this can be ascertained.

A printer who is definitely known to have been a regular priest is Arnold Therhoeren of Utrecht, who went to Cologne and was admitted to the university there on 4 May 1468. His purpose in

7. W. & L. Hellinga, *The Fifteenth-Century Printing Types of the Low Countries*, 2 vols. (Hertzberger, Amsterdam: 1966), vol. I, pp. 17–24.

*and helpe of almyghty god. whome I mekely supplye
to gyue me grace to accomplysshe hit to the playsir of
her that is cause therof and that she resseyue hit in gre
of me her faithfull trewe a moste humble seruant &c.
Thus endeth the seconde book.*

Type No 1 (from *The Recuyell of the Histoires of Troye*).

*Ja commence la controuersie de noblesse
platdoyee entre Publius Cornelius Sa-
pion dunepart. Et Gapus flammius de
autrepart. Laquelle a este faicte et compo-
see par un notable docteur en loyx et grant
orateur nomme Surse de pistoye.*

Type No 2 (from *La Controversie de Noblesse*)

*Explicit liber teraus: et opus rhetorice facultatis p fra
tre laurentiu Guikelmi de Saona ordinis minoru sacre pa
gine pfessore ep dictis testimonijsq3 sacratissimaru scriptu-
raru, doctoruq3 platissimoru compilatu g 9firmatu: quibus
ep causis censuit appellandu fore Margaritam eloquentie
castigate ad eloquendu diuina acomodatam*
*Compilatu auf fuit hoc opus in alma uniuersitate Can
tabrigie, Anno dni, 1478, die et, 6, Julij, quo die*

Type No 2* (from *Fratris Laur. Gul. de Saona*)

CAXTON'S TYPEFACES

In one respect, his choice of types, Caxton was not an enterprising man and from
his first year as a printer to his last, 1474 to 1491, a period of eighteen years, he was
content to use much the same founts as those he started off with in Bruges. The
types he brought from Cologne in 1472 were the old gothic sorts, and though the
first roman types were cut in 1467 at Strassburg and were perfected by Nicholas
Jensen in Venice in 1470, the unimaginative Caxton disregarded these avant-garde
designs completely. A possible reason is that as the gothic faces he favoured were
closer to the manuscript texts that his books were meant to compete with they
would appeal more to the wide public he sought.

Blades distinguishes six different founts as being used by Caxton, but as two of
these appear also in modified versions he contends that effectively Caxton used
eight separate castings. The modification of Type No 2 he distinguishes with an
asterisk as No 2*, and that of Type No 4 as No 4*. What Blades calls Type No 6 is
also strictly a modification of No 2.

O The moost swettest spouse of my soule Cryste
Jhesu desyryng hertely euermore for to be with the in mynd
ce and worshyp/ And to lete none erthely thynge be soo nyhe
myn hert as thou Cryste Jhesu/ And that I drede not for to deye
for to goo to the Cryst Jhesu/ And that I may euermore saye bn
to the with a gladde chere/ My lord? My god?/ my souerayne sauy-
our Cryst Jhesu / I byseche the hertely/ take me synner bnto thy
grete mercy and? grace/ For I loue the with al my herte/with all
my mynde/with alle my myght/ And? no thynge soo moche in erth
nor aboue erthe/as I doo the my swete lord? Cryst Jhesu / And?
for that I haue not loued? the/ and? worshipped? the/aboue al thyng
as my lord?/My god?/and my saueour/Cryst Jhesu/I byseche the
with mekenesse and? herte contryte / of mercy and? of forgeuenesse
of my grete bnkyndenesse/for the grete loue that thou sheldwest for
me and? al mankynde/What tyme thou offredest thy glorpous body
god? and? man bnto the Crosse/ther to be crucyfyed? and? woūded

Type No 3 (from *Death-bed Prayers*)

C Fynysshed and translated out of frensshe in to englysshe the
biij day of Juyn the yere of our lord M iiij C lxxvj / and
the first yere of the regne of kyng harry the bij/ And enprynt-
ted the xj day of Maye after/ at

Laus deo

C Thus endeth the doctrinal of sappyence the whyche is ryght
vtile and prouffitable to alle crysten men/ whyche is translated
out of Frensshe in to englysshe by Wyllyam Caxton at westme
ster fynysshed the .bij. day of may the yere of our lord / M /cccc
lxxix ix

Caxton me fieri fecit

Type No 5

Type No 1 is the most distinctive and is supposed to be based on the hand of
Colard Mansion, Caxton's partner in Bruges, who was a skilled calligrapher. It
was used for the printing of the *Recuyell* in Bruges and also for printing Lefevre's
original version from which Caxton made his own translation, *Le Recueil des
Histoires de Troye*. Type No 2 was the first type used in England when Caxton set

¶ Here after foloweth the mater
and tenour of this said Booke ✝
And the Fyrst chapyter saith to u
the good Heremyte deuysed to the
Esquyer the Rule & ordre of chy
ualrye

Contrey ther was
in which it happed that
a wyse knyght whiche
longe had mayntened
the ordre of chyualrye
And that by the force
& noblesse of his hygh
courage and wysedom
and in auenturyng his body had maynte=
ned warres Justes & tornoyes/ & in many
batailles And had many noble Byctoryes &
glorious/ & by cause he sawe & thouzt in his
corage þ he myzt not long lyue/as he which
by long tyme had ben by cours of nature
nygh vnto his ende/ chaas to hym an her=
mytage / For nature faylled in hym by
age / And hadde no power ne vertu to vse

A iij

Type No 4* (from *Order of Chivalry*)

up, and like 2*, 4, 4* and 6 has much the same character as Colard Mansion's "gros
bâtarde" type. Type No 3 and No 5 are not unlike those used in Mainz by early
printers of Bibles and psalters, and approach more than any other of Caxton's
types to what modern printers call "black letter".
    Blades relied on the differences he could discern between the types used in

n this tretyse that is clepd Go
uernaple of helthe: What is to
be sayd wyth crystis helpe of so=
me thynges that longen to bodi
ly helthe/hadde and to be kept or
to bodily helthe .lost and to be recouered/and
is departed in viij.chapptures/that is to saye
In the fyrste chapptre of the profytte of goode
Gouernaple of helth/In the ij.chapptre What
is first on morow to be don/In the iij.chapitre
of bodyly epcerspce/that is to saye. kefynes &
his profyte, In the fourth chapptre of spyces
of epcercice/In the fyfthe chapiptre how a man
sholde haue hym in mete.in etyng his metes :
In the vj.chapitre how a man shold haue hym
in drynkyng of his drynkes/In the vij.chap
ptre what sholde be done after mete/In the viij
chapptre of the noyse of euyll gouernaunce

It nedyth hym that woll haue longe
lyff to knowe the crafte of holsome go=
uerneple. And so for to kepe contynuelly the
helthe of his body/ for els he maye not com to

A i.

Type No 6

Caxton's various books to arrive at an estimated date of their printing, where Caxton does not give this. Blades' fallacy in this method of deduction was that he supposed that Caxton discontinued using one type when he acquired a new one – which surely no printer has ever done – and for this reason some of the dates he suggests are quite erroneous.

going to Cologne was to learn to print, and he was probably sent on that mission by his brethren in order to enable him to set up a press for them in the Netherlands. Though he became a member of the university at Cologne it would not be as such that he learned printing; even today a faculty of printing is a novelty provided by only a few universities. Instead he, like Caxton, is supposed to have been taught by Zell. But Therhoeren belonged to an order known as the Brothers of the Common Life, who had a house at Weidenbach, a suburb of Cologne. Also at Cologne were monasteries belonging to the Crutched Friars and the Carthusians. All three of these had supposedly taken up printing, and it is likely that Therhoeren went to the house of his own order to learn printing, rather than to Zell.

A reason advanced to support the notion that Caxton was taught to print at one of these convents is that a community of unworldly monks would be more willing to pass on the secrets of the trade than would a layman who was engaged in it for profit. He could, it is argued, have gone to Cologne armed with an introduction from the Benedictines at Ghent. His hosts at Ghent may not however have been Benedictines at all, but Brothers of the Common Life, who might have been loosely referred to as Benedictines because the rule adopted by most orders was based on that of St Benedict, to which slight changes were made to provide for particular aims. It may be significant that in his Chess book, printed at Bruges when these things were still clear in his memory, Caxton refers to the monks at Ghent as "White Freris" – which could be taken for "Freres" or "Friars". It is unlikely that he meant the latter, but if he did he is by no means the only person to have been careless in distinguishing between monks and friars.

Friars were either mendicants or preachers, and as such were free to wander abroad and were not the sort to take up a settled occupation like printing. For that reason the supposition already noted that the Crutched Friars at Cologne had a print shop is open to doubt. Incidentally the Crutched Friars wore a habit with a cross on it, and 'crutched' is a corruption of "crossed" – from the Latin word *crux*. It is much more probable that the house at Ghent was Carthusian, as the monks of this order wear a habit entirely of white. The fully professed members lived almost a hermit's life, each of them occupying a separate cell where they prayed, studied, slept and ate alone, emerging only to attend vespers, the night office and mass in the main chapel. Only on Sundays and saints' days did they feed together and enjoy a brief period of conversation. A discipline like this would not have permitted them to take up a corporate pursuit such as printing. The lay brothers of the order on the other hand, who looked after the bodily needs of the monks, worked in the gardens or on the abbey farm or at crafts of various kinds, one of which could well have been printing. Caxton's acquaintance with the monks at Ghent – whatever their persuasion was – could have stemmed from his having supplied them with cloth or he might even have bought manuscripts from them. And though we have agreed that at that time they would know nothing of printing, they could have facilitated his approach to the Carthusians in Cologne.

The idea however that Caxton learned printing at a religious house is no more than speculative. It is a possibility which we have duly examined, but the stronger one is that he received tuition from a lay printer. In spite of Blade's rough treatment of Wynken de Worde's statement that Caxton had something to do with the first printing of *De Proprietatibus Rerum* and learned his craft in the shop where it was produced, modern opinion is that de Worde was correct. Another work published in Cologne about the same time is *The Flowers of St Augustine,* and this has been attributed to the printer of the Cologne *De Proprietatibus Rerum,* largely because of the similarity of the type used in both of them. In a note on the latter in the British Museum catalogue mentioned earlier, L. A. Sheppard refers to "The Printer of the Flores S. Augustini who taught Caxton the art of printing at Cologne". From this he appears to have few reservations as to who taught Caxton. Furthermore he argues it was none other than Johannes Velderer, the man who supplied Caxton with his first founts of type. His actual words are: "It is possible on typographical grounds that the Printer of the Flores S. Augustini who taught Caxton the art of printing at Cologne is to be identified with Johann Velderer who matriculated at the University of Louvain on 30 July, 1473, and completed his first book in that city towards the autumn of the following year."[8]

8. Quoted by James Moran in his introduction to the 1971 reprint of Blades 1877.

In the final analysis we can be no more certain how or from whom Caxton learned the craft he adopted as a second calling than we can of most other aspects of his life. Blades denied that it was in Cologne, but his views have since been decisively overruled, and though we have to leave a number of other questions unanswered, we do know that Caxton arrived back in Bruges late in 1472 with enough knowledge of the techniques of printing to lay the foundations of a successful business in which he would be engaged for the rest of his life.

In Bruges Caxton lost no time either in showing the *Recuyell* to Margaret or, having obtained her approval, in putting into operation the final phase of the plan he had conceived in March 1468 when he first started on his translation with the firm intention of printing it. We have already questioned his statement that he printed the work merely to give copies to his friends, but Blades has no reservations on this. He says: "The manuscript translation made by Caxton for the Duchess of Burgundy, having excited great interest, a demand arose for copies quicker than Caxton could supply them. The printing press having been just established in that city by Colard Mansion, Caxton, whose thoughts were now homewards, determined to use it as a means of multiplying his translation, and of learning at the same time a new trade which would support him on his return to England."[9]

Blade's conviction that Caxton could not have learned to print in Cologne amounts almost to an obsession, and he devotes many pages to it. He bases his arguments mainly on differences that are to be found between the typographic styles employed in Cologne and those in the earlier books produced in Bruges. The difference he made most play with was that the Cologne school spaced out the lines of type in their books to an even length. Ulrich Zell appears to have started the practice in 1467, and Blades makes the point that if Caxton had learned to print in Cologne he would have brought the habit to Bruges with him, whereas it was not until 1479 that it was adopted by Mansion, and not until 1480 by Caxton, years after he had settled at Westminster. But is this as conclusive as Blades would have us believe? Early printing was no more than an attempt to reproduce manuscripts mechanically, uneven line endings as

---

9. Blades 1877 p. 168.

well, and when Zell and others began to square-up the type-area on their pages this was probably regarded as an unnecessary innovation. It was certainly not taken up universally.[10] Even today there are still typographers who maintain that irregular lines are not only easier to set and permit of more even word-spacing, but also assist the eye in reading. The great Eric Gill was a disciple of this.

In the previously quoted passage Blades quite plainly has no doubt that it was Mansion who taught Caxton to print. Today the opposite is known to be the case.[11] Blades went so far as to say that Mansion was the first printer west of Cologne and that he set up his press in Bruges soon after 1470, a year before Caxton left for Cologne. He implies not only that Caxton came back from Cologne without any knowledge of printing, but that Caxton got Mansion to print his translation for him. A noted French bibliographer and a contemporary of Blades, made a totally unsubstantiated suggestion that Mansion and Caxton were fellow-students of printing at Cologne.[12] Blades does not go along with this, but he very conveniently omits even to hazard a guess as to where Mansion was able to learn the craft and so anticipate Caxton. He contents himself with saying: "Mansion who had obtained some knowledge of the art of printing, although certainly not in Cologne, had just begun his typographical labours at Bruges, and was ready to produce copies by means of the press, if supported by the necessary patronage and funds. Caxton found the money, and Mansion the requisite knowledge, by the aid of which appeared *The Recuyell,* the first book printed in the new type, and moreover the first book printed in the English language."[13]

Blades was responsible of course for correcting many of the assumptions made by his predecessors, and his own findings for the most part still hold good. But on the subject of the relationship between Caxton and Mansion his theories went wildly astray. That Caxton entered into some kind of partnership with Mansion cannot

10. L. A. Sheppard, *A new light on Caxton and Colard Mansion* (Signature, New Series xv, 1952, pp. 28–39).
11. Sheppard, op. cit.
12. J. P. A. Madden, *Lettres d'un Bibliographe*, 4th Series (Paris: 1875), pp. 12–18.
13. Blades 1877 p. 68.

be doubted, and in doing so he displayed his usual good judgement. Mansion was a man of note in his native Bruges and a prominent member of the Guild of St John, a fraternity not unlike the Stationers' Company in London. It was given a charter by the book-loving Philip the Good in 1454, and its membership covered scriveners, illuminators, vignette painters and wood-engravers, makers of parchment and vellum, curriers and bookbinders. Later it was to enrol printers.

In 1471 Mansion was elected dean of the guild. Besides being an expert calligrapher and translator he ran a successful business as a bookseller. As such he would be in close touch with the market that Caxton hoped to enter, and in all probability Caxton had already had dealings with him and had perhaps bought manuscripts from him for export to England. It would be natural for Mansion to seek to extend his business by joining Caxton in his book printing venture, and to continue on his own as a printer when Caxton returned to England. He evidently lacked Caxton's acumen however, and ran into financial difficulties. From 1476 onwards he did not pay his dues to the Guild of St John. In 1480 he was reduced to seeking advances from a patron who commissioned him to produce an illuminated manuscript; receipts he signed for these exist. He also fell behind with the rent for the two rooms over the porch of the church of St Donatus where he had his workshop. It was here that in May 1484 he finished his magnificent edition of Ovid's *Metamorphoses,* a folio of nearly four-hundred leaves with numerous woodcuts – the cost of which ruined him. Faced with bankruptcy he left Bruges and disappeared. History has nothing further to tell of poor Colard Mansion.

But in 1472 Mansion was just the man to assist Caxton in printing his *Recuyell,* as well as in supervising the business when Caxton was away – for as we have noted, Caxton though no longer Governor of the Merchant Adventurers was still actively engaged on diplomatic missions right up to 1475. Just when Caxton and Mansion became partners is not known. It may not have been until after the *Recuyell* was printed, or even after *The Game and Playe of the Chesse* appeared. Neither of these carry the name of the printer, the place where they were printed, or a date, but as they are both in English it is likely that Caxton had a greater part in their production than the four books in French that are attributed to the Caxton-Mansion partnership.

As Caxton did not get back from Cologne until the end of 1472 it was probably early in 1473 that he set up his press in Bruges, and as the *Recuyell* is a work of considerable length it would, in view of the primitive nature of early presses, have taken some months to complete the printing of it. Moreover as Caxton would not have an abundance of type it is likely that he could compose only a page or two at a time and would then have to break these up after running them before proceeding with the next pages. It is obvious too that the dedication to the Duchess Margaret could have been written only after he had returned to Bruges and shown her his translation, and the same goes for his prologue and epilogues. For these reasons it is usually accepted that the date of its publication was late 1473 or even early 1474. Blades, himself a practical printer and aware of the problems that would face Caxton, plumped for the later date but placed a question mark after it.

The same arguments largely apply to the Chess book. According to Steinberg Caxton translated this from the Latin of Jacobus de Cessolis,[14] though Blades had already demonstrated, with his impressive bibliographical grasp, that Caxton had used a French version made by Jean de Vignay about the middle of the fifteenth century. Through the good offices of his patron Margaret he obtained permission to dedicate this book to her brother, George duke of Clarence, again no doubt hoping that this would prove a good sales gimmick. Caxton says that his translation was "Fynyssid the last day of marche the yer of our lord god a thousand four hunderd and lxxiiii . . ." So apart from being engaged in printing the *Recuyell* Caxton would seem to have busied himself with preparing a second translation for publication, having presumably overcome the inhibitions that he professed to labour under when working on his *Recuyell*. This would also suggest that he would need assistance with the printing of the *Recuyell* and that he had already taken on Colard Mansion as a partner. A pitfall which has led to the mis-dating of many books printed at this time is pointed out by Blades. He mentions that in the Low Countries it was then

14. S. H. Steinberg, *Five Hundred Years of Printing* (Pelican Books, London: 1955), p. 102.

A Blacksmith from *The Game and Playe of the Chesse* (1481?)

CAXTON'S USE OF WOODCUTS

In fifteenth-century England wood engraving was not as advanced as on the Continent, and perhaps the reason why Caxton did not incorporate illustrations in his earlier works was that he could not obtain the services of a suitable artist. Later he was more fortunate and as can be seen from the examples on this and the following pages the strikingly dramatic effect that could be gained with this primitive medium is quite remarkable. His first tentative use of woodcuts was in the third edition of *Cato* (1481?) which included two. These he also used later in the same year in *The Mirrour of the World* but added a further thirty-two designs. In the second edition of *The Game and Playe of the Chesse* (also 1481?) sixteen woodcuts appear, eight of them being used twice, in different chapters. For the next two years Caxton did not employ any woodcuts but when he resumed using them in 1484 graphic techniques had greatly improved. This is apparent from the examples here, from *The Fables of Aesop* and the second edition of *Canterbury Tales*. Both these books contain numerous woodcuts, the style of which suggests they are by the same hand. This unacknowledged artist was probably responsible also for the engravings in Caxton's *magnum opus* and the most lavishly illustrated of his works, the *Golden Legend,* which contains the largest woodcuts used by Caxton; one showing "The Assembly of the Saints" measures 9 × 6½ inches. His smallest are the four illustrations in the text of *Speculum Vitae Christi* (1488?), but in spite of that they have immense artistic vigour.

Caxton's smallest woodcuts, from *Speculum Vitae Christi* (1488?)

The Wife of Bath from the second edition of *The Canterbury Tales* (1484)

from *The Fables of Aesop* (1484)

Iherome is layd of
Ihera that is hooly / And
of nemus / that is to saye a
wood / And soo Iherome
is as moche to saye as an hooly wood

St Jerome from the *Golden Legend* (1484)

the custom to count the year as beginning on Easter Day. In 1474 this fell on 10 April. Thus Caxton 'fynyssid' his translation of the Chess book not in 1474 but on 31 March 1475. Allowing once more for the time that would be required for setting the type and for printing the pages one by one, as was the general practice (though Zell from an early period printed pages two-up[15]), Blades gives the date for the publishing of the Chess book as 1475–76, but again adds a question mark.

Caxton was always a prodigious worker, and in the period from his arrival back in Bruges at the end of 1472 to the time he left for England in 1476, his press produced four, possibly five, other books in addition to the two just discussed. Even if he had the help of Colard Mansion this was a remarkable output in the course of just three years. The book about which there is some doubt as to whether it was printed in Bruges or not until after he started his press at Westminster, is the *Propositio clarissimi oratoris magistri Johannis Russell*, the Latin discourse delivered at the investiture of Charles the Bold with the Garter on 4 February 1470. As this could hardly be expected to command a good sale, which was an important criterion in Caxton's choice of titles for publication, its printing was more than likely commissioned by its venerable author. Because the other four were in French, Blades and others insisted that they must have been printed either by Mansion on his own or possibly by Mansion with the assistance of Caxton, pursuing the notion that Mansion was Caxton's teacher.

Great emphasis was made of the fact that the first of these French works was Lefèvre's original from which Caxton had translated his *Recuyell* – namely *Le Recueil des histoires de Troyes*. This could be thought to be in direct contradiction of Caxton's plan to specialise in English publications. But was it? For Caxton the overriding consideration was to *sell* books – an exciting new commodity of which he had great hopes. Neither the size of the market for books in those days nor the production methods then available would permit of editions running to the number that can be disposed of nowadays. He could expect to sell some of his printing of the *Recuyell* to members of the English community in Bruges, and the rest through his existing connexions in London. For French books

---

15. Blades 1877 pp. 62–63.

however there was another, much larger, market immediately to hand in Bruges itself, where French was the *alter lingua*. So why not, he can be heard to reason, print a few books in French? It was not his intention just yet to return to England; in any case his duties as the king's factor would keep him in Flanders for a few more years. If his partner Mansion did not himself suggest cashing in on the French market, he would no doubt agree with the idea, and was in a position to recommend and supply suitable manuscripts.

The remaining three books that came from the press at Bruges were *Les fais et proesses du noble et vaillant chevalier Jason* (another work from the pen of Raoul Lefèvre), *Septenuaire des pseaulmes de penitence* and *Les quatres choses derrenieres*. There is no knowing in what order they appeared, but de Ricci dates them all 1475–6.[16] None of them has the printer's name, the place or a date. In his notes on *Jason* Blades dates it simply '147–?' – but then proceeds to argue, again riding his hobby-horse about uneven lines, that both this book and the *Seven Penetential Psalms* must have been printed by Mansion after 1478, when Caxton had departed. Seemingly unaware of any inconsistency he dates the English translation of *Jason* which Caxton made and printed in England as appearing in 1477(?) – as also does de Ricci – and even suggests that it actually pre-dates Earl Rivers' *Dictes*, now universally acknowledged to be the first book printed in England. The *Dictes* is certainly the first English book to carry a definite statement of the place and date of its production: "Enprynted by me William Caxton at Westmestre the yere of our lord Mcccclxxvij." If therefore Caxton's English version of *Jason* was printed in 1477 – even allowing for Blade's ubiquitous question mark – he must have been in possession of a copy of the French original or of the Bruges edition of it. And if he made his translation from the latter a reasonable conclusion is that he had a hand in printing it and that this was while he was in Bruges.

In the same way Blades has no hesitation in ascribing *Les quatres choses derrenieres* to "Mansion alone or assisted by Caxton" and dates it 1476(?). He admits however that close similarities exist between this book from the Bruges press and the English translation by Lord Rivers produced by Caxton. The printing of this –

---

16. S. de Ricci, *A Census of Caxtons* (Bibliographical Society, London: 1909).

WOODCUT INITIALS FROM CAXTON'S BOOKS

Until as late as 1485 Caxton employed a lettering artist or "rubrisher" to insert on his printed sheets the initial letters at the beginning of chapters when he thought these necessary. After 1484 he adopted woodcut initials and used them more and more frequently. Most of them are purely functional and straightforward in design, but some are much more decorative than others, as these examples show. The foliated A at bottom right is one of the first woodcut initials Caxton used, and appears in both *Aesop* and in *The Order of Chivalry*.

Cordyale or *The last four thinges*, as it is called – was completed on
"the xxiiij daye of Marche in the xix year of Kyng Edwarde the
fourthe" – in other words 24 March 1478. As with the Chess book
Blades corrects this date, to 24 March 1479 (with which de Ricci
concurs) because of the custom already mentioned of reckoning
years as starting on Easter Day. More important still is Blades'
admission that *Cordyale* is "an accurate reproduction, line for line
and almost word for word, of the French edition."[17] Again therefore it is reasonable to conclude that Caxton was closely concerned
with the production of the earlier French version in Bruges. Today,
in spite of Blades' lengthy discursions on the relative claims of
Mansion and Caxton, it is now accepted that Caxton was the prime
mover in bringing the art of printing to Bruges, was the principal
partner of the Bruges press, and was responsible for the production
not only of the *Recuyell* and the Chess book but also of the four
books in French which Blades denied to him.

---

17. Blades 1877 pp. 183 and 215.

CHAPTER 11

Westminster

If the date 1475–6 which has been ascribed to the four French books that Caxton printed in Bruges is to be relied on, he would appear to have been hard at work right up to the moment he packed his type and equipment to return to England. This we can deduce from the fact that by the end of 1476 he had completed all the formalities of finding premises in Westminster and had settled in sufficiently to be able to print an indulgence – on the sole surviving copy of which the date 13 December 1476 has been added by hand. This indulgence granted by Pope Sixtus IV, was issued by John Sant, abbot of Abingdon (where there was a daughter house of the great Benedictine abbey of Westminster) to a Henry Langley and his wife. For it to be dated by hand indicates that it had been printed earlier and the date added only when it was actually issued. Caxton could well therefore have arrived back in England as early as the summer of 1476.

The Langley indulgence, though it is the earliest known product of Caxton's Westminster press, may not in fact have been the first, as it is not a job that would take much time to set and run off. Moreover the time lag between Caxton's return and 18 November 1477, when the much lengthier *Dictes* by Earl Rivers was published, is great enough to suggest that Caxton would not have left his press idle throughout that period. This is borne out by the evidence of Robert Copland, one of Caxton's assistants who later started up on his own – "following the trace of my mayster Caxton, begynnyge with small storyes and pamfletes". Caxton would be involved in no personal outlay or risk in printing the Langley indulgence and his 'reward' for it would be immediate.

In between producing his major works Caxton appears to have more than once supplemented his income by printing indulgences and six such jobs, dated variously between 1480 and 1489, have been found. It was the reproduction of indulgences and their distribution in large numbers, which was made possible by the printing press, that was later to lead to Martin Luther's denunciation of them. As the successor of St Peter, to whom Christ had committed the keys of the kingdom of God, the Pope might well claim the power to remit the punishment due for sins, providing the sinner was truly penitent. But in course of time indulgences, the instrument of remission, came to be hawked around by 'pardoners' who were often themselves evil-living men and would part with an indulgence to anybody who had ready cash, or would even use them as stakes on a throw of dice.

Why Caxton chose Westminster and not London as the place to set up his press has been endlessly debated by his biographers. The City in which he had served his apprenticeship as a mercer was the business hub of metropolitan London, where he still had useful connexions, and it could be supposed that he would naturally gravitate to his old haunts. The reason he did not was thought to be that the stationers and professional copyists who were already entrenched there would not welcome a printer, whose 'black art' might threaten their livelihood. This hardly holds water; as a freeman of the most important of the city livery companies he could easily have overcome any such objection. In any case printing was at first regarded as complementary rather than competitive to the stationers' trade and later the two would be merged.

Blades, in a great flight of fancy, suggests that Caxton went to Westminster because of the great wool staple that had grown up there, and he gives a detailed account[1] of the lavish dinner which the Mercers' Company held in 1477 at the Greyhound Tavern in honour of the staplers who supplied them with their principal raw material, wool – which would be brought from Caxton's native Weald by road to the south bank of the Thames and then across the river by ferry. Of this festive occasion, which cost the mercers 28s 8d, and 2d for washing the table-cloth, Blades says that "if not there by right as a liveryman of the Mercers Company, the printer would be a welcome guest". "Surely", he goes on, "before parting, in remembrance of past associations and services one of the drink-

---

1. Blades 1877 pp. 76–79.

Anthony Woodville, Earl Rivers, presenting his *Dictes* to Edward IV, from a
manuscript in Lambeth Palace Library. Sitting with the king is his queen, Elizabeth
Woodville – Rivers' sister – and standing beside them is their elder son, the future
Edward V, to whom Rivers was tutor. Standing on Rivers' left is Richard duke of
Gloucester, later Richard III. The figure kneeling beside Rivers was once thought
to be William Caxton, but in view of his clerical dress and tonsure is now
considered to be a scribe called Haywarde, who made a fair copy of Rivers'
translation for him and possibly drew this illumination.

ing pledges would be 'The health of William Caxton, late governor of our fellowship beyond the sea'."

Another popular theory explaining why Caxton settled at Westminster was that he had family connexions there. We have already mentioned the William Caxton who was buried at St Margaret's in 1478 and who could perhaps have been the printer's father[2]. The parish records also show that in 1474 an Oliver Cawston was buried there, but no one has ventured an opinion as to what degree of relation he might have been to the partner[3]. In the accounts of the Guild of Our Lady for the years 1474–77 a John Caxston is shown as having paid 6s 8d on becoming a member. And the Abbey records show that a Richard Caxston or Caston was a monk there from 1473 until his death in 1504[4]. In 1490 the burial took place at St Margaret's of Maude Caxston who might have been the printer's wife. This she could well have been, and the fact that Caxton was married is proved by a manuscript dated 29 May 1496 which was found in 1874 among a collection of Exchequer rolls in the Chapter House at Westminster and which is now in the Public Record Office. It is a judgment given in a matrimonial dispute between Gerard Croppe, merchant tailor of Westminster and Elizabeth his wife – who is specifically described as "the doughter of William Caxton"[5]. Elizabeth Croppe is the only person of whose relationship with Caxton there is documentary proof; the others can only be regarded as possibly being relations of his, and even if they were, this would not account for his setting up his business among them.

The simple truth is that Caxton shrewdly chose to start up as a printer in Westminster because that was where he would find a ready market for his books and other publications. The merchants in the city of London were literate men and might be expected to buy some of his output, but he could look for far greater sales among the leisured members of the royal court at Westminster. He was already known to the king, and even without the letters and recommendations that he probably had from the king's sister,

2. v.s. p. 37.
3. Blades 1877 p. 158.
4. E. H. Pearce, op. cit. p. 165.
5. Blades 1877 pp. 163–4 prints the document in full.

Margaret of Burgundy, he would be given ready admission to court circles. The courtiers were all likely customers for the tales of chivalry and the poetry which he had in mind to produce. At Westminster there was also the Abbey and with the patronage of the abbot he could look to the church authorities for other regular work for his press – not only modest jobs like indulgences, but more substantial and more profitable volumes – service books like the Sarum Ordinale, which he produced within a year of setting up at Westminster, psalters, collections of sermons, lives of the saints and books of private devotions.

It was through the agency of the Abbot of Westminster that Caxton obtained premises in which to set up his press. This would be John Esteney, who was appointed abbot in 1474. Stow was well off the mark in his *Survey* when he wrote: "Islip, Abbot of Westminster, erected the first Presse of booke printing that ever was in England about the yeare of Christ 1471. William Caxton citizen of London, mercer, brought it into England, and was the first that practised it in the sayde abbey".[6] John Islip did not become abbot at Westminster until the year 1500 when he was promoted from the daughter house at Abingdon, and his able administration is commemorated by the street just behind the Tate Gallery which is named in his honour. Stow's statement however that Caxton practised printing "in the sayde Abbey" was for a long time taken to mean that his press was actually within the fabric of the abbey. Blades rightly pours scorn on this idea. "It has been argued", he says, "that Caxton was permitted by the abbot to use the Scriptorium of the abbey as a printing office. Printing, even in these days of improvement, is necessarily in some parts a very unclean operation, but it was much more so in its earlier years, some of the processes employed being extremely filthy and pungent. The Abbot of Westminster would never have admitted into the scriptorium anything so defiling, much less within the sacred walls of the church itself. There is, indeed, no evidence that any portion of the abbey was ever appropriated as a scriptorium: no mention of such a place is made by any historian, nor has any manuscript been recognised as having issued thence".[7] In saying this Blades is only

---

6. C. L. Kingsford's edition (1908), vol. ii, p. 122.
7. Blades 1877 p. 74.

partly correct. It is true that no manuscript of any note can be attributed to the monks of Westminster, but the work of copying and illuminating was practised in all major religious houses and a very accurate manuscript map drawn in 1755 by Henry Keene, the abbey surveyor, plainly shows a scriptorium situated on the north side of the Great Cloister.[8]

An even more outrageous but widely held idea was that Caxton's press was first set up in the very sanctuary of Westminster Abbey. This the abbot would have been even less likely to permit than in the scriptorium, for by definition the sanctuary is "the part of a church round the altar: an inviolable asylum, refuge, a consecrated place which gives protection to a criminal taking refuge there".[9] When it is said that Caxton had his press in 'the sanctuary at Westminster' it is necessary to understand what was meant by the expression. In theory a fugitive could take sanctuary in any church, but in practice it was possible for his pursuers to blockade the church and starve him out. Certain large churches and abbeys however had special privileges relating to sanctuary, and offenders were safe if they managed to place themselves within a prescribed distance of these buildings. Westminster Abbey was one of them and its rights had been clearly defined since the days of its founder, Edward the Confessor. Sanctuary at Ripon and Beverley extended in a circle a mile in radius around the minsters in these two towns. The bounds of sanctuary at Westminster it is not now easy to establish, but clearly they must have encompassed a good measure of ground, and the area was known as the Westminster City of Refuge – an allusion to similar havens set up by the ancient Israelites as described in the Book of Numbers, Chapter 35.

Walter Besant devotes an entertaining chapter to the subject of sanctuary and to an imaginary encounter with John Skelton, the self-styled poet laureate who was well known to Caxton, and whose name Caxton cunningly works into his translation of the *Eneydos* as a testimonial to the book's courtly prose.[10] Skelton, from being a humble parish priest in Norfolk became tutor to the future Henry VIII and a protegé of Wolsey's, but later lost the

8.   Westminister Abbey Muniments 34508 D.
9.   Chambers's Dictionary.
10.   op. cit. chap. VI.

Cardinal's favour by writing lampoons and scurrilous verses about him and had to take refuge from the tyrannical prelate's vengeance, ending up as a 'sanctuary man' at Westminster. Skelton's opinion of his fellow sanctuary birds, in the words Besant puts into his mouth, is a low one: "murderers, house-breakers, cutters of purses, common thieves, who come to save their necks, and all day long plot new crimes, which by night – stealing out privily – they commit, bringing hither their stolen goods, then there are the unthrifts, who, when they have spent their all, buy things for which they cannot pay, and bring them here to live merrily upon them while they last. The wife comes here laden with her husband's plate, saying that the good man beats her, so that to live with him is intolerable. Then she sells the plate, and God knows what manner of life she leads here." Besant also makes Skelton say of Caxton "he printed books of mine", but this is misleading. Earl Rivers, Benedict Burgh, John Lygate and Malory were the only English authors who were Caxton's contemporaries and were published by him, if we disregard smaller pieces such as John Russell's *Propositio* and some sermons by John Mirk (*Festial*). Skelton is certainly not numbered among Caxton's authors.

Sanctuary was denied to no one except Jews, infidels, traitors and those guilty of sacrilege, and if sanctuary was violated those guilty of such an affront to the church were liable to excommunication and heavy fines. When the traitorous upstart Perkin Warbeck, whom Margaret of Burgundy, Edward IV's sister and Caxton's patron, had put up to impersonating her late brother's murdered son, Richard duke of York, the younger of the 'Princes in the Tower', fled to Beaulieu Abbey after his rebellion failed, Henry VII respected his claim to sanctuary. This could be not so much clemency by Henry, but an instance of his political insight, in that the new king wished to demonstrate that he was ruler by right of descent from Edward III, even if only by way of the illegitimate Beaufort line, and that he had no need to fear pretenders. Only when Perkin left Beaulieu of his own accord and started plotting again did Henry's patience give out, and the misguided lad was hanged at Tyburn.

Elizabeth Woodville, Edward IV's consort and sister of Caxton's friend and first author, Earl Rivers, twice took sanctuary at Westminster. The first time was in 1470 when Edward fled to Bruges[11] and it was in sanctuary that Edward's first son was born. The second occasion was in 1483 when her husband died, largely of dissolute living, though he was only forty-one. Like most men of his class Edward led an adventurous sex life, and acknowledged one bastard son, while gossip credited him with two baby girls who were born to ladies of his court. Though he did not neglect his marital duties towards Elizabeth (they had ten children in all) he blithely admitted his infidelities. The most notorious of his mistresses was Jane Shore, wife of William Shore, a prominent mercer and a close friend of Caxton – as is seen from the fact that in 1487 he gave Caxton and two other friends power of attorney over his entire goods and chattels[12].

It would be diverting to think that it was through Caxton in some way that Edward first met Jane Shore, though perhaps this would be stretching imagination too far, because in March 1476 Jane was apparently no longer living with her husband and was petitioning for an annulment of her marriage on the grounds that her husband was 'frigidus et impotens'. She evidently found adequate consolation with Edward, who at the end of his reign was openly maintaining her – a situation which was tolerated by the queen, who accepted with almost a show of friendship the vivacious little woman who kept her husband amused. Even Sir Thomas More had a good word for her: "The king would say that he had three concubines which in three divers properties diversely excelled. One the merriest, another the liveliest, the third the holiest harlot in his realm. The merriest was this Shore's wife."

Though an able king and always popular Edward later developed an easy-going and self-indulgent streak and left matters of state more and more to his industrious younger brother, Richard duke of Gloucester, for whom he had a great affection and after whom he named his second son. The result was that when Edward died on 9 April 1483 the administration was already effectively in the hands of Richard, who lost no time in declaring himself regent. Edward's elder son, by right the new king Edward V, was at Ludlow with his maternal uncle, Earl Rivers, who had been appointed his 'governor'

11.   v.s. p. 110.
12.   Calendar of Close Rolls, Hen. VII, 203.

and mentor. On the news of Edward IV's death Rivers set off for London with his young charge, but Gloucester intercepted them at Stony Stratford. Rivers was sent north under guard to Pontefract Castle, and there on 25 June 1483 Caxton's first author and friend was beheaded without even a mockery of a trial, along with Sir Thomas Vaughan and Richard Grey, Elizabeth Woodville's son by her first marriage.

Gloucester was out for the blood of the Woodville faction, and Elizabeth, fearing for her own safety and that of her second son, Gloucester's namesake, hurried from the palace at Westminster to the adjoining City of Refuge, together with her five surviving daughters. Gloucester had lodged young Edward in the Tower 'for his safety', without allowing him to see his mother – in fact he would never see her again in this life – and before long, with the connivance of Archbishop Rotherham, who casuistically agreed that a blameless child had no need of sanctuary, Gloucester took the other boy from his mother's custody and sent him to keep his brother company in the Tower. Gloucester justified his actions by arguing that during the minority of the new king the government of the country could not be left in the hands of the queen mother, who anyway had no experience in such matters. It was not long before his true intentions became clear. With the aid of another clerical toady, Robert Stillington, bishop of Bath and Wells, he put it about that Edward IV's marriage with Elizabeth Woodville was invalid and their entire brood of children, including the supposed new king, illegitimate. In fact, announced Gloucester, the throne was rightfully his own, and ruthlessly he liquidated the few remaining peers who opposed him or whom he thought likely to oppose him. On 6 July 1483, three months after the death of Edward IV and only three weeks after the execution of Rivers, Gloucester was crowned as Richard III.

It was no time for heroic gestures. Caxton, who owed much to Elizabeth Woodville and still more to her brother, could only grieve privately over the loss of his friend and patron and the sorry plight of the doubly bereaved queen. There was nothing that Caxton could do to assist her, and his own well known association with her brother required him to be circumspect in his attitude towards the usurper who now had the throne. The situation also created business problems for him, and these he had to set about trying to resolve. He had lost his principal patron, who could have been expected to back him in the production of *The Golden Legend*, a lengthy account of the lives of the saints which he was then busy compiling from a variety of French, Latin and English manuscripts. It was an expensive undertaking, but by the end of this year of woeful events he was able to announce publication. He had managed to obtain the support of William Fitzalan earl of Arundel, a crony of Richard's, who though he showed no interest in any of Caxton's subsequent works promised to buy a 'reasonable quantyte' of this particular book and offered Caxton a 'yerely fee' of a buck in summer and a doe in winter'.

The drastic change in circumstances at court does not in fact appear to have affected Caxton's publishing programme to any serious extent, though he had to make some last minute alterations to the prologue or dedication of some of the books he brought out in Richard's reign. For instance, he finished translating *The booke whiche the knyght of the toure made* on 1 June 1483, right in the middle of Richard's bid for power, and publication had to be delayed. It is now easy to explain why. When the *Knight of the Tower* finally appeared on 31 January 1484 Caxton said in the prologue that it had been translated "at the request of a noble lady which hath brought forth many noble and fair daughters." Caxton was a great namedropper if he considered that the mention of a titled person would help to sell a book, but in this case he had second thoughts apparently.

It is not difficult to identify the anonymous 'noble lady' as Elizabeth Woodville – who certainly brought forth many daughters.[13] But it would have been rash indeed for Caxton to have done so. Caxton was equally cautious when he printed the *Curial* (1484?), in which he contents himself with saying that he had translated it "for a noble and virtuous Erle" – presumably Rivers. Caxton, despite his inner feelings, was anxious to curry favour with the new king, so much so that when he issued a second edition of *The Game and Playe of the Chesse*, which Blades dates '1481?' but de Ricci post-dates to 1483, he discreetly omitted the original dedication to

---

13.   N. F. Blake, *The "noble lady" in Caxton's "The Book of the Knyght of the Towre"* (Notes and Queries, ccx, 1965) pp. 92–93.

'George duc of Clarence', for by then it was widely believed that Richard had had a very active hand in the death of Clarence, who a few years previously had been up-ended in a butt of Malmsey wine in the Tower. Obviously Richard would not want to be reminded of the occurrence. With *The Booke of the ordre of chyvalry* Caxton turned his coat completely. This work is usually dated to 1484, and though its translation was commissioned by 'a gentyl and noble Esquyer', who could have been an adherent of the Woodvilles, Caxton shamelessly dedicated it to Richard "my redoubted lord and king".

When Elizabeth Woodville and her family took refuge from Richard duke of Gloucester it would not be in the actual sanctuary, the area around the high altar, of Westminster Abbey – any more than it was there that William Caxton set up his press. The narrower definition of sanctuary is a post-Reformation, even modern, limitation of the meaning of the word, and, as we have said, in Caxton's time the Sanctuary at Westminster was an extensive area outside the Abbey itself. It was mainly on the north side of the Abbey and was bounded roughly by what is now Great George Street, taking in and including the present Parliament Square to the east and stretching to the beginning of Tothill Street on the west. Today there are reminders of its extent in the name of the block of professional offices adjacent to the Abbey's west door, which is called The Sanctuary, and in the names of the street called Little Sanctuary running behind the Middlesex Guildhall and of Broad Sanctuary, the bombed site near the Methodist Central Hall which thirty years after World War II has still not been built on and now serves as a car-park.

It was on this particular spot, some fifty or sixty yards from the north-west corner of the Abbey, that there stood a forbidding thick-walled structure of stone seventy-five feet square and sixty feet high, not unlike the central keep of a castle. It had but one door of heavy oak with plates of iron, and on the lower floor one closely barred window. The upper story, reached by a winding staircase in a narrow circular tower, had a few more barred windows, but little air and less of God's light reached the gloomy interior of this depressing edifice – which was St Peter's Sanctuary, the hub of the Westminster City of Refuge. It was here that Edward IV's widow sought safety and here that Richard III dragged her younger son from her arms. This grim medieval relic, though it ceased to be recognised as a sanctuary after the Reformation, remained standing until 1775.

The old Palace of Westminster whence Elizabeth Woodville fled stood where the Houses of Parliament now are, between the east end of the Abbey and the river, and today the seat of government is still called the Palace of Westminster. But long before a palace was built at Westminster there was a monastery or minster. The name West Minster first occurs in a charter by which King Offa in 785 authorised the building of a monastery on 'Thornéa', a desolate island of about forty acres formed by two outlets of the Tyburn stream, with a man-made ditch joining them in the west, while the Thames served as the eastern boundary of the island. The southern outlet of the Tyburn ran the length of what is now Great College Street and in Caxton's day turned the wheel of the Abbey Mill, while the northern one roughly followed the line of today's King Charles Street and Derby Gate, entering the Thames about four hundred yards downstream. Great Smith Street and Storey's Gate now lie on what was the course of the cross-ditch.

The Thames in those days was a broad and shallow tidal estuary with marsh and swamp land on either side, and Thorney Island as it was known and is still so called on some maps, was an infertile fen where only monks seeking solitude and a life of self-denial would choose to settle.[14] This first West Minster was later destroyed by Danish raiders, but on its site Edward the Confessor laid the foundations of the great Abbey we know today. Successive kings added to its splendour. The nave was enlarged by Edward I, Henry V donated the Chantry, and Henry VII erected as his sepulchre the 'sumpteous and solempne chapel' that bears his name, which with its fan-vaulted ceiling, more like filigree than masonry, is one of the jewels of our architectural heritage. The twin towers over the west door were built by Wren or maybe by his pupil Hawksmoor; they were certainly not there in Caxton's time, and in the picture which Besant and others use of Caxton's supposed house in the Almonry.

---

14.   Strictly "Thorney Island" is tautologous. "Thorn-ey" by itself means "Island of Thorns". v.s. p. 66.

they are an obvious anachronism.[15] Without these the Abbey, when Caxton lived in its shadows, must have been a squat and much less imposing building.

The nature of its terrain made Thorney Island a natural stronghold which could be easily defended in troublous times. Recognising this King Canute (1017–35) built himself a stockade there, on the side of the Thames and not far from what remained of the primitive monastery. Twenty years or so later Edward the Confessor, having re-established the Benedictines on the island, converted Canute's stockade into a royal lodging. Being himself more monkish than regal in his way of living he simply wanted to be near his beloved Abbey, but more worldly kings built on and added to his modest dwelling and the Palace of Westminster became the most favoured of royal residences.

In most respects the royal household was self-sufficient, and the Palace housed in addition to the royal family and its attendant courtiers a small army of functionaries and menials. But to complement these other services were required, and around the Palace numerous tradesmen and artificers established themselves, built substantial homes and no doubt prospered. At the same time there grew up, to the west and north-west of the Abbey, an insalubrious slum of narrow streets and mean hovels which remained in being for centuries, until the construction of Victoria Street in the middle of the nineteenth century cut a broad swath through them. This was the Westminster City of Refuge to which John Skelton betook himself. The Palace and the Abbey divided between themselves the whole of Thorney Island, with the respectable people who served the royal household and enjoyed its patronage living cheek by jowl with the sanctuary rabble who huddled together under the protection of the Abbot.

The oldest part of the Palace that has survived is Westminster Hall, the walls of which are those originally built by William Rufus between 1097 and 1099. Rufus called his building the New Hall to distinguish it from the great hall of Edward the Confessor's Palace which lay slightly to the south. Nine centuries later the yard at the north of it is still known as New Palace Yard. The Westminster Hall we know today is substantially the same as it was in the reign

15.   op. cit. p. 181.

F

of Richard II, though the handsome hammer-beam roof suffered damage in an air raid on 10 May 1941. It was not only the Great Hall – the principal apartment – of the royal household but from the earliest times was also the meeting-place of the Great Council, from which grew the Courts of Justice and Parliament. By 1300 the Courts of King's Bench, Common Pleas, Exchequer and Chancery were all held here, and they remained at Westminster until 1882, when the present Royal Courts of Justice were opened in the Strand.

Here we have a clue as to the location of the first premises that were occupied by William Caxton when he set up as a printer in Westminster. Just opposite Westminster Hall, near the apse of Henry VII's 'sumpteous and solempne chapel', there is a modern ironwork gate which replaced a postern in the wall that formerly separated the Palace from the Abbey precincts. Beyond this gate a path runs alongside the wall of the chapel and past Poets' Corner to a door leading into the south transept of the Abbey. As however Henry VII's chapel was not completed until 1500 it should be remembered that in Caxton's time the path would run beside the Old Lady Chapel which then formed the east end of the Abbey. The path is spanned by one of the flying buttresses of the Chapter House, but in spite of its proximity to the Abbey fabric this path or narrow street was not hallowed ground and was given over to secular purposes. Like St Paul's Churchyard it contained 'stations' or stalls and even more substantial business premises which were rented out. In the Sacrist's accounts for the year 1476–7 appears the entry:

De alia shopa ibidem dimisso Willelmo Caxton . . . Xs

or in other words 'For another shop in the same place let to William Caxton . . . 10s'.[16] This should not be taken to mean that Caxton was taking a *second* shop; the reference to 'another shop' relates to the entry immediately preceding this one, which is in respect of a letting to an unnamed tenant for a half year at a rent of 5s. The Sacrist's accounts provide the first documented evidence of where and when Caxton started printing at Westminster, for as the rolls run from one Michaelmas to the next it is probable that he took possession on or about 29 September 1476, which would give him

16.   Westminster Abbey Muniments 19724. cf. Crotch 1928 p. ciii.

A fifteenth-century Parliament of the Lords Temporal and Spiritual.

good time to print the Langley Indulgence which is handdated 13 December 1476. Caxton continued in fact to rent this and adjoining shops until his death in 1491, when the original shop was taken over by Wynken de Worde. The spot is now marked by a commemorative tablet to Caxton which was unveiled in November 1954 outside the Poet's Corner door mentioned above, in appreciation of the assistance given by the Press in promoting the Abbey's Appeal for £1,000,000.

The grounds for this being the actual location of Caxton's first printing shop were established by Lawrence E. Tanner, Keeper of the Muniments at Westminster Abbey, in a paper presented to the Bibliographical Society on 21 February 1956.[17] The Sacrist's accounts refer specifically to the shop near the Chapter House and prove that Blades and most other biographers were wrong in assuming that it was in the Almonry that Caxton started off. Stow's assertion that Caxton practiced printing 'in the sayde Abbey' was decisively disposed of by Blades himself, as we have noted. Blades accepts however Stow's statement that Caxton's first tenement was in the Almonry, considerably to the west of the Chapter House. After describing the monastery and the Palace Stow says: 'Now will I speake of the gate house, and of Totehill streete, stretching from the west of the Close . . . On the Southside of this gate, king H. the 7. founded an Almeshouse . . . Neare unto this house westward was an old chappel of S. Anne . . . The place wherein this chappel and Almeshouse standeth was called the Almory, for that the Almes of the Abbey were there distributed to the poore.'

In St Ann's Street, off Abbey Orchard Street, there is still today a church of the same name on the site of the 'old chappel of S. Anne', and this helps to pin-point exactly the former location of the Almonry. 'The position of both St Anne's Chapel and the Almonry, in relation to that of the Abbey Church', comments Blades, 'seems to have been misunderstood by all of the biographers of Caxton. Dr Dibdin, Charles Knight and others, place them on the site of the Chapel of Henry VII, which is the east end of the Abbey'.[18] If they do, it is a remarkable coincidence that they antici-

---

17.   Published in *The Library*, 5th series, xii, 3, September 1957, pp 153–66.

18.   Blades 1877 pp. 72–74.

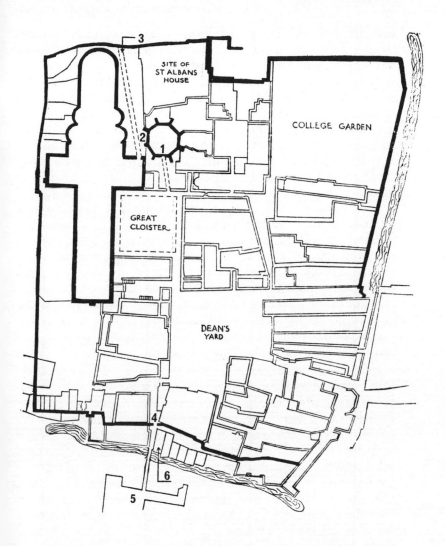

The precincts of Westminster Abbey, adapted from Keene's manuscript map of 1755 and showing (1) the Chapter House, (2) the site of Caxton's first shop, (3) the postern and pathway leading to the door in the south transept of the Abbey, (4) the gate through to the Almonry, (5) the site of the Almonry, and (6) the site of Caxton's second house.

pate Tanner's findings by over a century in their attempts to fix the location of Caxton's first house in Westminster, even if they are wrong in deciding just where the Almonry lay.

Though Tanner, with the aid of the Sacrist's Account Rolls, has shown that we can with certainty say that Caxton's first press at Westminster was adjacent to the Chapter House, he himself appears to go curiously astray when he goes on: 'it was not until some years later, either in 1482 or 1483, that he took in addition to his original shop the premises in the Almonry usually known as the Red Pale.' He makes the point that the majority of Caxton's earlier books are described by him as 'emprynted by me William Caxton in thabbey of Westminster', whereas later books are said to be printed simply 'at Westminster'. On the basis that *The History of King Arthur* was 'Emprynted in thabbey of Westminster, the last day of July the yere of our lord Mcccclxxxv' he goes so far as to suggest that the press was not moved to the Almonry until 1485. In this he follows Blades, who not only makes a similar distinction between the imprints of the books produced in this period, but decides that the expressions 'in the Abbey of Westminster' and 'at Westminster' evidently refer to the same locality, 'for otherwise we must suppose Caxton to have carried on two separate printing-offices for many years'.[19] To both Blades and Tanner the idea that Caxton could have occupied two lots of premises would seem to be unthinkable. But is it? The *Advertisement* with which Caxton sought to promote the sales of the *Sarum Ordinale* invites customers to 'come to West-monester in the almonesrye at the reed pale', and as the *Ordinale* was produced in 1477, or possibly 1478, it is plain that Caxton must already have had a place of business at the sign of the Red Pale in the Almonry as well as near the Chapter House.[20]

In another instance also Tanner could be misleading. He quotes from the account roll of the Almonry for the year 1482–3 this entry, which is also quoted by Crotch[21]:

De Camera sup(ra) portam exteriorem nuper de D(avid) Selley ad T(erminum) xl annorum hoc a(nn)o xxxvj jam in tenencia Willi Caxton per annum . . . iijs iiijd

19.   Blades 1877 pp. 70–71.
20.   Plate 00.
21.   Crotch 1928 p. clvii.

The Sign of the Red Pale

Jf it plese ony man spirituel or temporel to bye ony pyes of two and thre comemoracios of Salisburi vse enpryntid after the forme of this preset lettre whiche ben wel and truly correct, late hym come to westmonester in to the almonesrye at the reed pale and he shal haue them good chepe ⁖

Supplico stet cedula

Caxton's Advertisement with which he sought to promote the sale of the *Sarum Ordinale*. As the latter was printed in 1477, this is evidence that Caxton already had a house "at the red pale" in the Almonry.

This house, which the entry says had been leased to David Selley for forty years of which there were thirty-six to run when Caxton took it over, is where Tanner says Caxton probably died in 1491. He then remarks: 'It is a curious fact that nowhere in our records is the "Red Pale" mentioned, in spite of Caxton's well-known exhortation to his customers to "come to Westmonester in the Almonestrye at the reed pale"'.

In other words he identifies this house rented in 1482 as the one over which the sign of the Red Pale was displayed, though the *Advertisement* shows Caxton to have been using the sign over a house in the Almonry as early as 1477–8. Plainly this is not the first house or the only one occupied by Caxton in the Almonry, and Tanner is on safer ground when he says of the Red Pale: "The explanation is, I think, that it was a personal trade-mark hung outside the house to attract attention, and was merely attached to the house during the period of his tenancy." This could well be, and is certainly more satisfactory than the suggestion that has been made that Caxton found the sign already in position and to it over with the premises.[22] There is no evidence at all that the sign was ever displayed over the house that Tanner has shown Caxton to have taken over from David Selley, but if he was already using it at the house he rented earlier elsewhere in the Almonry he could have taken it with him.

That the Red Pale was used by Caxton to designate his house was the belief of Blades, who tells us: 'The printers of the fifteenth century, especially in Holland and Flanders, very frequently used armorial bearings for their trade-marks, the shield being represented as hanging from the branch of a tree. A broad band down the centre of the shield is, in heraldic language, called a "pale", and this, if painted red, would be a "red pale". The printers at Delff, in Holland, used a "black pale" for their marks.'[23]

22. N. F. Blake, *Caxton and his World* (Andre Deutsch, London: 1969) p. 223.
23. Blades 1877 p. 76.

CHAPTER 12

Ars Moriendi

When Caxton chose to take premises near the Chapter House of Westminster Abbey he was using the same shrewd judgement that brought him to the neighbourhood of the royal palace in the first place. As we have said, the Great Hall of the palace was the meeting-place of parliament – or at least of the Lords, for until 1265 parliament consisted only of nobles. Even when the Commons did come into being they were not the democratic assembly we have today; only knights, landed gentry and certain burgesses were eligible and these were summoned by writ and not elected. In any case parliaments were originally called only when the king thought it necessary, or sensible, to consult his barons on matters of importance, such as the raising of exceptionally large taxes for the conduct of wars.

In the fourteenth century the practice grew up of the Lords and the Commons sitting separately, and it was this development that led Caxton to set up shop where he did. Then as today, when a parliament was summoned both Lords and Commons gathered first in the Great Hall for a "state opening", but afterwards the Commons would retire to their own chamber – the Chapter House of Westminster Abbey, easily accessible by way of the postern in the palace wall. The Chapter House in fact had been intended from the time of its erection to accommodate secular councils as well as monastic ones, and although for one period the monks managed to reserve it for themselves alone and compelled the Commons to meet in the Abbey refectory, even to reach this the members of the Commons still needed to use the path that went past Caxton's bookshop.

Caxton's choice of this site was a wise one, as is seen from the fact that in spite of his taking on other premises in the Almonry, he retained possession of his original shop right up to his death, and it was presumably because it was such a good investment that Wynken de Worde kept it on. The Sacrist's accounts show that Caxton also rented an adjacent shop for 2s 6d for the year 1483–4. Not only could he rely on a steady trade from members of the Commons passing to and from the Chapter House, but the south door into the Abbey was also used by the royal family and the courtiers when attending services there. It is conceivable therefore that he first came to the notice of Henry VII on such an occasion, for soon after the death of Richard III at Bosworth on 22 August 1485 Caxton was able, without apparent qualms, to accept the new king as "the most christian king, my natural sovereign lord."[1]

Later the Sacrist's roll for 1488–89 show Caxton to have rented a booth near the pathway at a cost of 4d for just one week. "in the time of the parliament." It is to this year that both Blades and de Ricci date Caxton's *Statutes of Henry VII,* the first ever volume of statutes to be printed. According to Blades the *Statutes* are "further remarkable as being in English", though in fact it was the often misjudged Richard III who first insisted that laws should be written in the common tongue. In securing this commission Caxton no doubt had in mind that the *Statutes* would especially appeal to the members of parliament who had assisted in framing them, but they represent his only venture into parliamentary printing. Henry, though in 1489 he requested Caxton to print *The Fayts of Arms,* was not a liberal patron and it was his mother, Margaret Beaufort, countess of Richmond, who became Caxton's principal backer in his latter years.

History shows Henry VII as a great pragmatist in matters of state, but coupled with his nobler traits was a cautious streak that amounted almost to parsimony. When in January 1486 he married Elizabeth, daughter of Edward IV and Elizabeth Woodville and niece of the man he had slain at Bosworth, it was for the laudable but purely practical purpose of uniting behind him the warring adherents of York and Lancaster. It is typical of him that his bride was to be recognised only as his consort rather than as having rights of her own as Edward IV's eldest surviving child.

---

1   Prologue to *The Fayts of Arms.*

He was not sparing however in his arrangements for her coronation, which he saw as a good piece of public relations. The procession that escorted Elizabeth from the royal apartments in the Tower to the west door of the Abbey must have been a spectacle of great pomp and splendour, and must have pleased the eyes of the ageing printer – who would be among the sightseers, or even present in the Abbey, as he was a citizen of consequence in Westminster by now and well known to the monks. Dressed in a gown of white silk damasked with pure gold thread, and an overmantle trimmed with ermine, the young queen (she was then twenty) was borne on a litter over which four knights held a canopy of cloth of gold, and behind which four peeresses in attendance on her rode on grey palfreys. Moreover for once the streets on the route had been swept clean of rubbish, and the houses along the way were all festooned with red cloth. Lining the streets were cheering crowds held in check by troops and retainers in bright tabards, and among them was the whole complement of the City's liverymen in their distinctive and colourful livery garb.

The first fruit of this union of York and Lancaster was born the following year. The baby prince is said to have been christened Arthur after the hero of the book that Caxton published on 31 July 1485, based on a manuscript that had been put together in prison "from certain books in French" by Sir Thomas Malory. Malory was once identified with a rascally Warwickshire knight who led a band of brigands and failed lamentably to live up to the chivalrous ideals that are extolled in *Morte d'Arthur*. This old villain has since been displaced as the author by a Yorkshire knight of the same name, and one critic has suggested that there are distinctly northern touches in the vocabulary of *Morte d'Arthur*.[2]

Perhaps Henry did, and perhaps he did not, name his son after the legendary King Arthur, but for Caxton a more certain and happy consequence of this political union was that it resulted in the re-instatement of what few remained of his old friends among the Woodville following, and he no longer needed to hide his former associations with them. Particularly he could now reveal without danger the affection he had had for the new queen's ill-fated uncle, Earl Rivers. In Richard III's reign he had felt obliged to refer only

2.   William Matthews, *The Ill-framed Knight* (University of California: 1966).

obliquely to Rivers when he printed the *Curial* in 1484, but in the third edition of Rivers' *Dictes* which appeared in 1489 Caxton felt it was safe to use again his noble patron's name.

It has been observed that the third edition, like the second edition which appeared in 1479 or 1480, is dated 1477 as was the first edition. This is not a case of unwitting ante-dating but an instance of the practice common among early printers of reprinting in all subsequent editions the colophon and date of the *editio princeps*. On one occasion Caxton did make a genuine mistake in dating a book. This was in Gower's *Confessio Amantis* where the colophon has the date "a thousand CCCC lxxxxiij." Fortunately he also included the regnal year – "the first yere of the regne of Kyng Richard the thyrd" – which fixes the true date of the book as 1483.

Though Henry VII was a luke-warm supporter of the press Caxton had no compunction in turning to advantage what slight acquaintance/he had with the king, and when in 1490 he published his *Eneydos,* a hotch-potch paraphrase of portions of Virgil's *Aeneid* from various French translations, he "presented" it to Prince Arthur, who was then but four years old. This he was able to do through the good offices of John Skelton, who had been appointed the prince's tutor. Caxton's praise of Skelton's literary style in the preface to *Eneydos* borders on the fulsome. He writes: "But I pray mayster John Skelton, late created poete laureate in the universite of Oxenforde, to oversee and correct this said book . . . for him I know for sufficient to expowne and Englysshe every difficulty that is therein. For he hath late translated the epistles of Tully, and the book of Diodorus Siculus, and diverse other works . . . in polysshed and ornate termes craftily . . . I suppose he hath drunken of Elycon's well."

None too subtle though this flattery is, it would no doubt go a long way in persuading Skelton to recommend acceptance of the book by his young charge, or on his behalf – and this Caxton perhaps hoped would be as good as an outright testimonial for it. That however could be taking too harsh a view of Caxton's motives. His own writings suggest that he sincerely admired and would be naturally attracted by Skelton's occasionally macaronic style and that he sought to imitate it. Whatever the explanation the *Eneydos* was not a best seller; it never went to a second edition and more copies of it have survived than of any of Caxton's works.

Though Caxton received no great support directly from the new king, any more than he did from Edward IV or Richard III, he was able to find other influential patrons and friends besides Skelton. The most gracious was Margaret Beaufort, the king's mother, at whose behest he translated *The History of Blanchardin and Eglantine* in 1489. In the prologue he describes Margaret as "my redoubted lady", and redoubted she surely was. As her surname indicates, she could claim royal descent – even if this was dubious, deriving as it did from John of Gaunt's liaison with Catherine Swynford. Margaret was Gaunt's great-granddaughter and daughter of John Beaufort, first duke of Somerset. Her uncle was Edmund Beaufort, the second duke, killed in the opening battle of the Wars of the Roses at St Albans in 1455.

When her father died in 1444 (surprisingly of natural causes in those violent days) she was a baby of no more than twelve months, and the ambitious William de la Pole, duke of Suffolk, was able to secure her as his ward. In no time at all he put her through a form of marriage with his son, aiming thereby to put his family in the queue for the throne, as Henry VI was as yet unmarried and had no heir. Suffolk's murder in 1450 freed her, but in 1455, while still only a child of twelve, she was married off to Edmund Tudor, earl of Richmond. By this marriage Margaret acquired a second, though still decidedly weak, link with the Lancastrian chain of succession – which eventually would be used to bolster up the claim of her own son, Henry VII, to be rightful king of England. For her husband was a half-brother of Henry VI and a product of the clandestine alliance that Henry V's widow, Catherine of France, had contracted with the scheming Welshman Owen Tudor.

Within a year Margaret's second marriage was over; Edmund Tudor died in 1456 without seeing the boy that Margaret, now thirteen years of age, bore him on 28 January 1457. In 1464 Margaret married a third time, and in 1473 yet again. When she commissioned Caxton to translate *Blanchardin and Eglantine* she was the wife of Thomas Stanley, earl of Derby, but in his prologue Caxton addresses her in her maiden title as "duchesse of Somercete." In all probability Margaret had known Caxton slightly, or known of him, for some years before this, for in the same prologue he says that the French manuscript which she asked him to translate was one that he himself had sold to her "longe to fore", possibly while he was still a merchant in Bruges.

In point of fact the extent of Caxton's relationship with royalty, or even with the nobility, has been consistently exaggerated by his biographers. Earl Rivers seems to be the only peer with whom he enjoyed a degree of close, though still respectful, intimacy – and this could in part be due to Rivers' consciousness of having himself begun life as the son of a humble knight. Though Blades says that Henry VII personally desired Caxton to translate and print *The Fayts of Arms,* it is more likely that Caxton did not receive the manuscript from the hands of the king himself but through an intermediary, John de Vere, earl of Oxford, to whom Caxton was known and at whose 'commandment' Caxton printed *The Four Sons of Aymon* round about this time. Judging from Caxton's sly remarks in the prologue of this book intimating that he had printed it without financial assistance the noble earl was no more open-handed than his royal master.

In the prologue Caxton also tells us that he had earlier translated for the earl "the lyfe of one of his predecessoures named Robert Erle of Oxeforde." Of this neither Caxton's translation nor any copy of the book – if it ever went into print – has survived, but in his dealings with de Vere Caxton was displaying a degree of ambivalence. On 12 August 1481 he had published in one volume three English translations from Cicero (Tullius or Tully as he was called in Caxton's time) – *De senectute, De amicitia* and the *Declamation of Noblesse.*

The latter two translations, *Of Friendship* and the *Declamation,* Caxton credited to John Tiptoft, earl of Worcester, who as Constable of England under Edward IV had arraigned and executed in 1462 de Vere's father on Tower Hill for his alleged part in an abortive pro-Lancastrian rising. Tiptoft's character is one of the many anomalies that mark the later Middle Ages in Europe; men of great learning and liberal culture, like the Medicis, were indescribably ruthless and barbaric in their political actions. Tiptoft was probably the most erudite man in England, but for all that he was regarded with detestation on all sides and gained the name "butcher of England." In the short-lived Lancastrian coup of 1470–71 he got his deserts, ironically at the hands of the man whose father he had judicially murdered nine years before. Warkworth's Chronicle records: "And then was taken the Earl of Worcester, which was arrested and arraigned before Sir John Vere, the Earl of Oxford, son and heir to the 'foresaid Earl of Oxford which was beheaded at the Tower Hill, as before written."[3]

Caxton cannot ever have met Worcester but he was full of extravagant praise for him. His words are: "In hys tyme flowered in vertue and cunnyng none like hym among the lords of the temporalitie in scyence and moral vertue." But when he goes on: "The axe then att one blowe cut off more learnyng than was left in the heads of all the survyvyng nobilitie," Caxton was evidently unaware of the story that went around of how Tiptoft as he knelt at the block requested with superb aplomb that his head should be cut off with three strokes, in honour of the Holy Trinity.

The first piece in this volume, *Of Old Age,* was at one time thought to be Tiptoft's work also, but it cannot reliably be ascribed to any author. Caxton's prologue tells us that the translation was made at the ordinance and desire of Sir John Fastolf. This Fastolf has been treated unkindly by history, especially in that he was for long considered to be the prototype of Shakespeare's Falstaff. Blades in his comments on *Of Old Age* falls into that error when he says: "Literary taste is not often associated with the name of Sir John Falstaff."[4] No two characters could be more dissimilar than Shakespeare's buffoonish creation and the real-life Fastolf, who albeit he had a few setbacks, served with distinction throughout the campaigns of Henry V and of John duke of Bedford, retiring only in 1440 when he was past sixty, and then living to a ripe old age.

Like Worcester he was something of a bilateral personality. A servant said of him: "cruel and vengible he hath ever been, and for the most part without pity and mercy."[5] But unlike Worcester he does not appear to have had himself any aspirations to write, though he was evidently well-read. In addition to ordaining the translation of *De senectute* he commissioned in 1450 a translation of *Les dits moraux des philosophres,* long before Earl Rivers essayed this

3   J. C. Giles, op. cit. p. 119.
4   Blades 1877 pp. 189 and 230.
5· Paston Letters, i, 389.

task, and it is quite probable that Caxton's author leaned heavily on this when labouring on his *Dictes*. This translation is preserved in a manuscript in the British Museum and describes itself as "late translatyd out of frensh tung in to englysh the yer of our lord M ccccl to John Fostalf for his contemplacion and solas by Stevyn Scrope squyer sonne in law to the seide Fostalle."[6]

Not all of Caxton's patrons were persons of quality. It is true that in his earlier works he sought the patronage of royalty in the person of Edward IV's sister Margaret and through her of George duke of Clarence, and that the author of the first book he published in England was Edward's brother-in-law, but even at this early stage he was not above printing *Parvus Catho* and *Magnus Catho,* which, he says, "hath been translated out of Latin into English by Master Benet Burgh." Comparatively this Benet, or Benedict, Burgh was by Caxton's apparent standards a nobody, a minor churchman. We have, however, encountered his name before. He was vicar of Malden in Essex and is mentioned in the Little Wratting charters. When Caxton returned to England Burgh was a canon at Westminster, and we have already suggested that it was not by mere chance that he came to know Caxton and was able to prevail on him in 1477 to publish his *Cato*.

Conceivably he could have been a brother of Richard Burgh, the mercer who took livery at the same time as Caxton and who like Caxton was fined for not attending the riding of the new mayor, Geoffrey Fielding, on 13 October 1453. In any case Caxton was taking no great risk in publishing Burgh's poetic translation, for Cato's distichs in the original Latin had been popular for centuries. Moreover Burgh was a pupil, and later a literary collaborator, of John Lydgate, whose long poems commanded a wide following and could be relied on to sell well, a fact that Caxton was aware of when he published, also in 1477, Lydgate's *The Temple of Glass*. Caxton's speculation on Burgh was thoroughly justified. *Cato* went into a second edition within a year, and a third appeared in 1481.

Caxton had not approached his publishing venture as an amateur pastime; he was in it for business. When he wooed noble patrons his motives were unashamedly mercenary. Though he made unsparing use of the "humility formula" and might at times appear

---

6   MS Harley 2266.

almost sycophantic in his praise of anyone whose name he thought would help sell his books, basically he was no snob. He was a tradesman, and to the end of his days he was proud of his association with the City. When in 1483 he dedicated *Caton,* his own translation from a French version, "unto the noble, ancient and renowned City, the City of London in England" he was not fundamentally changing his attitudes, and when he describes himself in the same prologue as "of the fraternity and fellowship of the mercery" he indicates a fact that has sometimes been overlooked or denied – that he had always kept in close touch with his friends and former fellow-merchants.

It was not only his personal inclination and kindly disposition that would prevent Caxton from breaking with the past; to some extent the requirements of his printing business would require him to maintain ties with the Merchant Adventurers. For one thing he needed their services in obtaining, among other things, supplies of paper. Caxton made very little use of vellum, perhaps because he thought it was too expensive for the class of work he printed, and the paper he used was mainly imported from the Continent, where its manufacture by mechanical means, though these were still primitive, had been developed from the original Chinese manual methods of centuries before. The first paper maker in England was John Tate who died in 1514, and though he supplied the "paper thynne" on which Wynken de Worde printed his edition of Bartholemaeus' *De Proprietatibus Rerum* in 1498, the paper that Caxton used when he first started printing in England in 1476, and possibly throughout his printing career, had to be brought here by ship.

Nor did Caxton cast his own type. He was in fact most unadventurous in his choice of type designs and to the end of his days continued to use much the same founts as those he had started off with in Bruges. But when he did require to restock his cases he would have to buy type from the Continent, possibly from Johann Velderer at Louvain. Several generations of printers were to pass before there was an indigenous typefounding industry in this country. Moreover, besides printing books Caxton is known to have built up a considerable trade in imported books also. To obtain these he would again need the services of his merchant friends.

Apart however from commercial considerations there were some mercers who were always special cronies of Caxton's. There was Richard Burgh whom we have just mentioned and who may have been instrumental in his printing *Parvus Catho* and *Magnus Catho* for Benedict Burgh. Another of the mercers who like Richard Burgh and William Caxton was fined for not attending Geoffrey Fielding's riding was Thomas Bryce. The Mercers' Company appear to have been a tight-knit fraternity, and this Thomas was undoubtedly a brother or some relation of Hugh Bryce, for whom Caxton published *The Mirror of the World* as early in his printing career as 1481.

This disposes entirely of the allegation that Caxton lost the common touch and delighted only in the company of noble patrons. It suggests also that some of his mercer friends were more generous than his noble patrons, and that they sometimes took a financial interest in the production of some of his titles. For the publishing of *The Mirror of the World* was not a speculation that Caxton shouldered alone. In the prologue he tells us that it was undertaken "at the request, desire, coste and dispense of the honourable & worshipful man Hugh Bryce, alderman & citizeyn of London."

An especially close bond appears to have existed between Caxton and William Pratt throughout their lives. Like Caxton, Pratt was a native of Kent. Their indentures were registered in the same year, 1438; both took livery in the same year, 1453, and Pratt was also among the thirty-six liverymen who were fined for being absent from Geoffrey Fielding's riding. In another place it might be an entertaining investigation to try and discover why there were so many absentees on that occasion. Could it be that Fielding did not get on well with his fellow mercers or was an unpopular choice for mayor? Be that as it may, Pratt was another mercer who encouraged Caxton in his printing venture and like Hugh Bryce possibly co-operated financially in some of his publications.

The Book of Good Manners which Caxton 'enprynted the xi day of Maye' 1487 was produced "for a specyal frende of myn, a mercer of London named William Praat". Caxton's phraseology here so closely resembles the words he uses in certain other works that it has been suggested that Pratt might have had an interest in these also. When in 1478 Caxton printed Chaucer's translation of *Boethius*

De Consolatione Philosophae it was "atte requeste of a singular frende of old knowledge", and similarly the *Royal Book* or *A Book for a Kyng* (1484) was for "syngular frende of myn, a mercer of London". In view of the years separating these books it might be unsafe to say positively that the 'singular friend' in each case was William Pratt. But that Pratt was a life-long friend whom Caxton esteemed highly is certain, for it was on his death-bed that Pratt requested that *The Book of Good Manners* should be printed.

It is significant that from this time the thought of death appears to have been much in Caxton's mind, and an appreciable number of the books he undertook in the next five years either have this doleful theme or are religious works which aim at preparing man's soul for the life to come. Characteristically however he did not neglect to reprint several titles which had sold well and were standing in print, such as a second edition of the *Golden Legend* (1487) and of *Reynard the Fox* (1489), and a third edition of the *Dictes* (1489). He also translated and printed the romance *Blanchardin and Eglantine* for Margaret Beaufort, another romance *The Four Sons of Ayman* for John de Vere, earl of Oxford, and *The Fayts of Arms* at the 'request' of Henry VII.

The rapid succession of books that issued from Caxton's press from the time he turned to printing indicates the man's industry and application. The time he took over *The Fayts of Arms* however is exceptional; he appears to have spent something like eighteen months over it. Blades has an explanation for this. In 1490 died, and was buried at St Margaret's, one 'Mawde Caxton', of whose relationship to William Caxton there is no direct evidence. It may have been the Maude who, twenty-nine years earlier, became his wife while he was yet in Bruges; if so, it will explain, in a most interesting manner, the reason why he in that year suspended printing *The Fayts of Arms* until he had finished a new undertaking *The Arte and Crafte to Die Well*.[7]

In the vestry accounts of St Margaret's for the year 1490 is the entry:

Item atte Bureyng of mawde Caxston for torches and tapres iijs ijd

---

7 Blades 1877 p. 81.

Among the entries to be found in the accounts for the following
year is one that reads:

Item atte Bureying of William Caxton for iiij torches   vjs viijd
Item for belle atte same bureyng   vjd

Before the bell tolled for William Caxton he found time to translate
another "lytyll treatyse" for the comfort of those nearing death,
namely *Ars Moriendi; that is to say, The Craft for to Die for the Health
of Man's Soul.* But if he had any foreboding of his own death it did
not impair his intellectual vigour or his zest for work. Besides *Ars
Moriendi* he started on *Vitae Patrum,* his translation of *The Lives of
the Fathers.* He did not live to print it. This was done in 1495 by his
faithful assistant and successor in the business, Wynken de Worde,
who in the colophon to the book raised as fitting a memorial as
Caxton could possibly have wished. "Translated oute of Frenche
into Englisshe by William Caxton of Westmynstre late dead, and
finished the laste daye of hys lyff."

Some Background Books

Joseph Ames and William Herbert, *Typographical Antiquities, or an Historical Account of the Origin and Progress of Printing in Great Britain and Ireland,* 3 vols. 1785. (Revised edition, with notes, by the Rev. Thomas Frognall Dibdin, 1810).

H. S. Bennett, *The Pastons and their England* (University Press, Cambridge: 1922).

— *English Books and Readers 1475–1557* (University Press, Cambridge: 1952).

— *Caxton and His Public* (Review of English Studies, xix, 1943), pp. 113–19.

Walter Besant, *Westminster* (Chatto and Windus, London: 1895).

J. G. Birch, *William Caxton's Stay at Cologne* (The Library, 4th series, iv, 1923–24), pp. 50–52.

William Blades, *The Life and Typography of William Caxton,* 2 vols. (Trubner, London: 1861–63).

— *The Biography and Typography of William Caxton* (Trubner, London: 1877). 2nd edition, 1882. Reprinted 1971 with an introduction by James Moran (Frederick Muller, London).

— *How to Tell a Caxton, with some hints Where and How the Same might be Found* (Henry Sotheran, London: 1870).

N. F. Blake, *Caxton and his World* (Andre Deutsch, London: 1969)

— *William Caxton and Suffolk* (Proceedings of the Suffolk Institute of Archaeology, xxix, 2, 1962), pp. 139–53.

— *Two New Caxton Documents* (Notes and Queries, ccxii, 1967), pp. 86–87.

— *William Caxton and Suffolk: A Supplement* (ibid. xxx, 1, 1964), pp. 112–15.

— *The "noble lady" in Caxton's 'The Book of the Knyght of the Towre'* (Notes and Queries, ccx, 1965), pp. 92–93.

J. A. L. Calmette, translated by D. Weightman, *The Golden Age of Burgundy* (Weidenfeld and Nicholson, London, 1962).

Patricia Carson, *The Fair Face of Flanders* (E. Story-Scientia, Ghent: 1969).

Warren Chappell, *A Short History of the Printed Word* (Andre Deutsch, London: 1972).

Anthoney Cheetham, *Richard III* (Weidenfeld and Nicholson, London: 1972).

S. B. Chrimes, *Lancastrians, Yorkists and Henry VII* (University Press, Cambridge: 1964).

Mary Clive, *This Sun of York* (MacMillan, London: 1973).

W. J. B. Crotch, *The Prologues and Epilogues of William Caxton* (EETS, old series, 176, OUP, London: 1928).

Susan Cunnington, *The Story of William Caxton* (Harrap, London: 1917).

J. Gairdner, *The Paston Letters: 1422–1509* (Chatto and Windus, London: 1904).

J. C. Giles, *The Chronicles of the White Rose of York* (Bohn, London: 1843). Reprinted 1974 (A. J. Sutton, Dursley).

P. M. Handover, *Printing in London from 1476 to Modern Times* (Allen and Unwin, London: 1960).

W. L. Heilbronner, *Printing and the Book in Fifteenth-Century England* (University of Virginia Press, Charlottesville: 1967).

W. G. and L. Hellinga, *The Fifteenth-Century Printing Types of the Low Countries,* 2 vols. (Hertzberger, Amsterdam: 1966).

J. Huizinga, translated by F. Hopman, *The Waning of the Middle Ages* (Arnold, London: 1924).

P. E. Jones, *Calendar of Plea and Memoranda Rolls 1437–1457* (University Press,Cambridge: 1954).

N. J. M. Kerling, *Caxton and the Trade in Printed Books* (The Book Collector, iv, 1955), pp. 190–9.

Charles Knight, *William Caxton, The First English Printer,* 2nd edition (Clowes, London: 1877).

V. B. Lamb, *The Betrayal of Richard III* (Mitre Press, London: 1972).

John Lewis, *The Life of Mayster Wyllyam Caxton* (London: 1737).

K. B. MacFarlane, *The Nobility of Later Medieval England* (University Press, Oxford: 1973).

D. MacGibbon, *Elizabeth Woodville (1437–1492), Her Life and Times* (Barker, London: 1938).

James Moran, *Printing Presses: History and Development from the Fifteenth Century to Modern Times* (Faber and Faber, London: 1973).

A. R. Myers, *England in the Late Middle Ages* (Penguin Books, London: 1952).

— *The Household of Edward IV* (University Press, Manchester: 1959).

E. H. Pearce, *The Monks of Westminster* (University Press, Cambridge: 1916).

H. R. Plomer, *William Caxton 1424–1491* (Parsons, London: 1925).

A. W. Pollard, *The New Caxton Indulgence* (The Library, 4th series, ix, 1928–29), pp. 86–89.

G. Pollard, *The Company of Stationers before 1557* (The Library, 4th series, xviii, 1937–8), pp. 1–38.

Seymour de Ricci, *A Census of Caxtons* (Bibliographical Society, London: 1909).

L. F. Salzman, *English Life in the Middle Ages* (OUP, London: 1926).

C. L. Schofield, *The Life and Reign of Edward the Fourth*, 2 vols. (Longman, London: 1923).

William Seymour, *Battles in Britain*, Vol. 1 (Sidgwick and Jackson, London: 1975).

L. A. Sheppard, *A New Light on Caxton and Colard Mansion* (Signature, new series xv, 1953), pp. 53–56.

S. H. Steinberg, *Five Hundred Years of Printing* (Penguin Books, London: 1955).

R. L. Storey, *The End of the House of Lancaster* (Barrie and Rockliff, London: 1966).

L. E. Tanner, *Wiliam Caxton's Houses at Westminster* (The Library, 5th series, xii, 3, 1957), pp. 153–66.

A. H. Thomas, *Calendar of Plea and Memoranda Rolls 1413–1437* (University Press, Cambridge: 1943).

S. L. Thrupp, *The Merchant Class of Medieval London* (University Press, Chicago: 1949).

G. M. Trevelyan, *English Social History: A Survey of Six Centuries* (Longman, London: 1944).

H. F. Westlake, *Westminster, an historical sketch* (SPCK, London: 1919).

Index